I0448875

U.S. Department of Justice
Office of Justice Programs
National Institute of Justice

Hand-Held Metal Detectors for Use in Concealed Weapon and Contraband Detection

NIJ Standard–0602.02
Supersedes NIJ Standard 0602.01 dated September 2000
Supersedes NILECJ STD 0602.00 dated October 1974

Nicholas G. Paulter, Jr.
Electricity Division
National Institute of Standards and Technology
Gaithersburg, MD 20899

Prepared for:
National Institute of Justice
Office of Science and Technology
Washington, DC 20531

November 2003

NCJ 200330

National Institute of Justice

Sarah V. Hart
Director

This standard was prepared for the National Institute of Justice, U.S. Department of Justice, by the Office of Law Enforcement Standards of the National Institute of Standards and Technology under Interagency Agreement 99–IJ–R–094, Project No. 02–002.

The NIJ Standard–0602.02, "Hand-Held Metal Detectors for Use in Concealed Weapon and Contraband Detection," is a revision to and supersedes the NIJ Standard–0602.01 published in September 2000. The 2000 revision addressed concerns of the criminal justice and public safety communities for an updated performance standard based on current technologies and responded to recommendations from the Law Enforcement and Corrections Technology Advisory Council. This current revision responds to comments received from industry and the criminal justice and public safety communities on the 2000 revision.

K.D. Rice of the Office of Law Enforcement Standards (OLES) of NIST and D.R. Larson of NIST are acknowledged for their comments and recommendations.

FOREWORD

The Office of Law Enforcement Standards (OLES) of the National Institute of Standards and Technology (NIST) provides technical support to the National Institute of Justice (NIJ) program to support law enforcement and criminal justice in the United States. OLES's function is to develop standards and conduct research that will assist law enforcement and criminal justice agencies.

OLES is (1) subjecting existing equipment to laboratory testing and evaluation, and (2) conducting research leading to the development of several series of documents, including national standards, user guides, and technical reports.

This document covers research conducted by OLES under the sponsorship of NIJ. Additional reports as well as other documents are being issued under the OLES program in the areas of protective clothing and equipment, communications systems, emergency equipment, investigative aids, security systems, vehicles, weapons, and analytical techniques and standard reference materials used by the forensic community.

Technical comments and suggestions about this guide are welcome and may be addressed to the Office of Law Enforcement Standards, National Institute of Standards and Technology, 100 Bureau Drive, Stop 8102, Gaithersburg, MD 20899 8102.

Sarah V. Hart, Director
National Institute of Justice

CONTENTS

Page

FOREWORD iii
COMMONLY USED SYMBOLS AND ABBREVIATIONS vii
1. INTRODUCTION 1
    1.1 Purpose of the Standard 1
    1.2 Definitions 1
2. REQUIREMENTS FOR ACCEPTANCE 8
    2.1 Safety Specifications and Requirements 9
    2.2 Electrical Requirements 9
    2.3 Detection Performance Specifications 10
    2.4 Operating Requirements 11
    2.5 Mechanical Specifications and Requirements 14
    2.6 Functional Requirements 15
    2.7 Detector Holder 16
    2.8 Quality Control and Assurance 17
    2.9 Documentation 18
3. PERFORMANCE TESTING PROCEDURES 20
    3.1 General Test Conditions 21
    3.2 Detection Performance Tests 21
    3.3 Alarm Indication Tests 24
    3.4 Test for Operation Near a Metal Wall 25
    3.5 Battery Life Test 26
    3.6 Burn-In Test 26
    3.7 Power Cycling Test 26
4. FIELD TESTING PROCEDURES 27
    4.1 Large Object Size 27
    4.2 Medium Object Size 27
    4.3 Small Object Size 27
    4.4 Very Small Object Size 27
5. TEST OBJECTS DESCRIPTION 27
    5.1 Large Object Size Test Objects 27
    5.2 Medium Object Size Test Objects 30
    5.3 Small Object Size Test Objects 32
    5.4 Very Small Object Size Test Objects 40
6. COMPLIANCE TEST REPORT FORM 44
7. REFERENCES 44

FIGURES

Figure 1. Diagram of two different hand-held metal detectors showing the detector plane
   and the detector axis 2
Figure 2. Drawing of the detector holder and detector positioner showing attachment at
   the reference surface 3
Figure 3. Diagram of the measurement coordinate system showing the measurement coordinate
   system axes, one measurement plane, the detector plane, and the reference surface,
   where the detector holder, containing a detector, is unmounted 5
Figure 4. A schematic of the detector and the detector positioner, with detector in place,
   where the detector holder is properly located on the detector positioner; that is,
   where the z axis of the measurement coordinate system, the detector axis, and the
   reference axis are collinear; the detector holder and detector positioner are in
   contact at their reference surfaces; and the long axis of the detector is collinear with
   the x axis of the measurement coordinate system 6
Figure 5. Mechanical drawing of the reference surface 17

vi

COMMONLY USED SYMBOLS AND ABBREVIATIONS

A	ampere	H	henry	nm	nanometer
ac	alternating current	h	hour	No.	number
AM	amplitude modulation	hf	high frequency	o.d.	outside diameter
cd	candela	Hz	hertz (c/s)	Ω	ohm
cm	centimeter	i.d.	inside diameter	p.	page
CP	chemically pure	in	inch	Pa	pascal
c/s	cycle per second	IR	infrared	pe	probable error
d	day	J	joule	pp.	pages
dB	decibel	L	lambert	ppm	parts per million
dc	direct current	L	liter	qt	quart
°C	degree Celsius	lb	pound	rad	radian
°F	degree Fahrenheit	lbf	pound-force	rf	radio frequency
dia	diameter	lbf·in	pound-force inch	rh	relative humidity
emf	electromotive force	lm	lumen	s	second
eq	equation	ln	logarithm (base e)	SD	standard deviation
F	farad	log	logarithm (base 10)	sec.	section
fc	footcandle	M	molar	SWR	standing wave ratio
fig.	figure	m	meter	uhf	ultrahigh frequency
FM	frequency modulation	min	minute	UV	ultraviolet
ft	foot	mm	millimeter	V	volt
ft/s	foot per second	mph	miles per hour	vhf	very high frequency
g	acceleration	m/s	meter per second	W	watt
g	gram	N	newton	λ	wavelength
gr	grain	N·m	newton meter	wt	weight

area = unit^2 (e.g., ft^2, in^2, etc.); volume = unit^3 (e.g., ft^3, m^3, etc.)

PREFIXES

d	deci (10^{-1})	da	deka (10)
c	centi (10^{-2})	h	hecto (10^2)
m	milli (10^{-3})	k	kilo (10^3)
μ	micro (10^{-6})	M	mega (10^6)
n	nano (10^{-9})	G	giga (10^9)
p	pico (10^{-12})	T	tera (10^{12})

COMMON CONVERSIONS (See ASTM E380)

0.30480 m = 1 ft	4.448222 N = 1 lbf
2.54 cm = 1 in	1.355818 J = 1 ft·lbf
0.4535924 kg = 1 lb	0.1129848 N·m = 1 lbf·in
0.06479891 g = 1 gr	14.59390 N/m = 1 lbf/ft
0.9463529 L = 1 qt	6894.757 Pa = 1 lbf/in^2
3600000 J = 1 kW·hr	1.609344 km/h = 1 mph

Temperature: $T_{°C} = (T_{°F} - 32) \times 5/9$

Temperature: $T_{°F} = (T_{°C} \times 9/5) + 32$

NIJ STANDARD
FOR
HAND-HELD METAL DETECTORS FOR USE IN
CONCEALED WEAPON AND CONTRABAND DETECTION

1. INTRODUCTION

1.1 Purpose of the Standard

The purpose of this document is to establish performance requirements and testing methods for active hand-held metal detectors used to find metal weapons and/or metal contraband carried on a person and/or concealed by a nonmetal object.

1.2 Definitions

The definitions are provided to help the reader use and understand this document, which describes methods for evaluating active hand-held metal detectors used as weapons detectors. Terms that are defined here appear in *italics* in the remainder of this document.

All measurement units used in this document are metric. Length units are abbreviated: meter (m), centimeter (cm), and millimeter (mm). Where useful, English units are indicated in parentheses immediately following the metric units, such as "2.54 cm (1 in)."

1.2.1 Active Detector

An *active detector* is generally a device that generates energy for illuminating the target space. For the hand-held metal detector, the generated energy is in the form of a magnetic field. The interaction of this magnetic field with certain types of objects in the region around the detector and the ability to detect this interaction are the basis of operation for hand-held metal detectors.

1.2.2 Alarm Indication

A signal to warn of the detection of a metal object. The indication can be visual and/or auditory.

1.2.2.1 Positive Alarm Indication

The change in the *alarm indication* that corresponds to the detection of a metal object. Typically, the *alarm indication* is off until a metal object is detected.

1

1.2.2.2 Proportional Alarm Indication

An *alarm indication* proportional to the size, proximity, orientation, and/or material of an object.

1.2.3 Alarm Indicator

The device used to generate the *alarm indication*. This device can provide a visual, auditory, and/or vibratory indication. For a visual indication, the alarm generating device can be a light bulb, lamp, light emitting diode, etc. For an auditory indication, the alarm generating device can be a horn, siren, buzzer, or similar item.

1.2.4 Detection

The discovery or finding of a metallic object. The *detection* of a metallic object is transmitted to the operator by some type of *alarm indicator*, typically a visual or audible indicator.

1.2.5 Detector Axis

An imaginary line passing through and perpendicular to the *detector plane* that is located within the *detector plane* such that the magnetic field around the *detector axis* has the maximum symmetry. The *detector axis* is labeled as the "z" axis. The location of the *detector axis* relative to the detector shape and geometry is specified by the manufacturer. See figure 1.

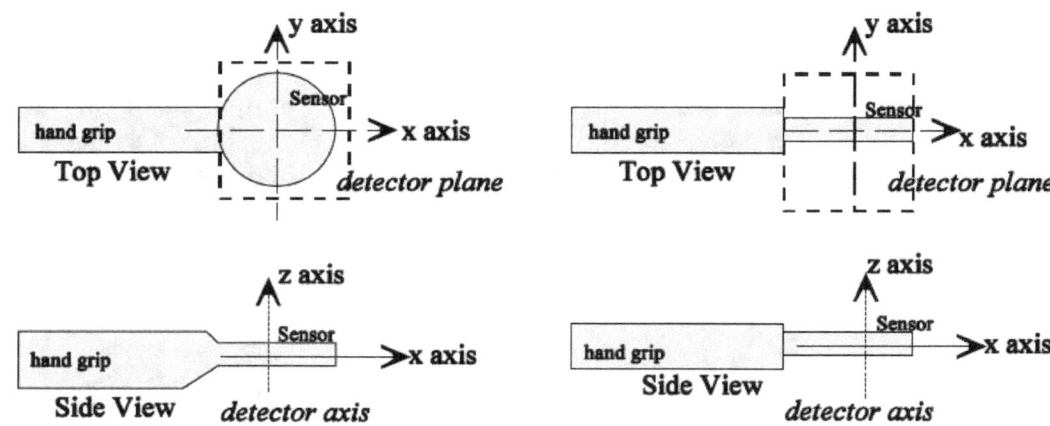

Figure 1. Diagram of two different hand-held metal detectors showing the detector plane *and the* detector axis

1.2.6 Detector Holder

A nonconductive, nonmagnetic block that holds the hand-held metal detector for testing. The *detector holder* is supplied by the manufacturer and contains a *reference surface* that mates to the *reference surface* of the *detector positioner*. Figure 2 shows how the *detector holder* is used and section 2.7 provides specific requirements.

1.2.7 Detector Plane

An imaginary plane (two-dimensional surface) that passes through the center of the sensor region of the hand-held metal detector, bisects the sensor region into two symmetric halves, and is parallel to the plane of the sensing element. The *detector plane* contains two orthogonal axes labeled as the "x" axis and as the "y" axis. See figure 1.

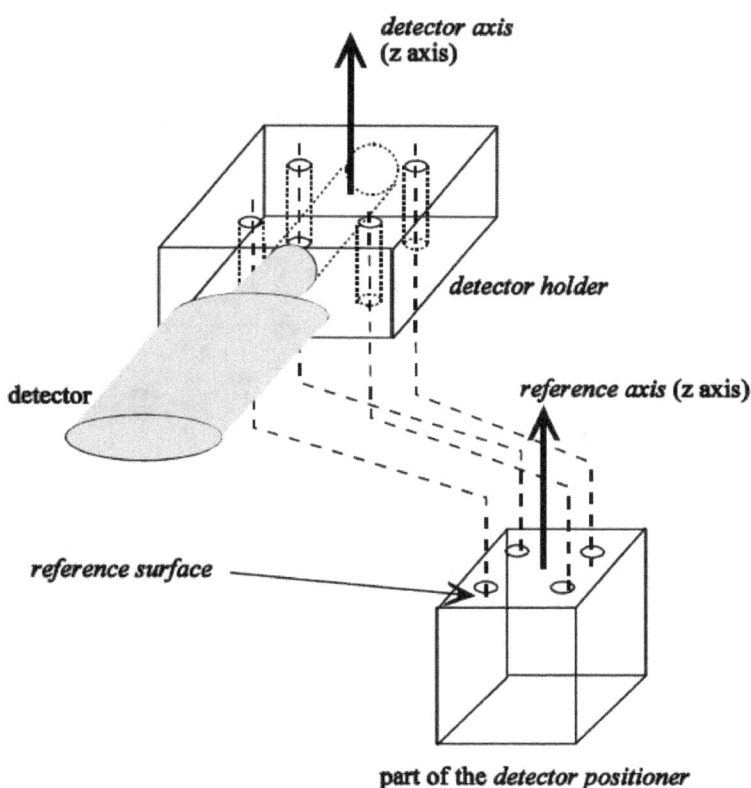

Figure 2. Drawing of the detector holder *and* detector positioner *showing attachment at the* reference surface

1.2.8 Detector Positioner

A nonconductive, nonmagnetic device that fixes the position of the *detector plane* and *detector axis* with respect to the *three-axes translation system*. The *detector positioner* includes a *reference surface* for attaching the *detector holder*. The *detector positioner* also includes a surface for attachment to the *three-axes translation system*.

1.2.9 Detector Response

The electrical signal generated by the sensor or sensor circuit of the detector that is caused by an object interacting with the magnetic field generated by the detector. The *detector response* is the basis on which an *alarm indication* is derived.

1.2.10 Measurement Coordinate System

A mutually orthogonal three-dimensional Cartesian coordinate system referenced to the *detector axis* and the *detector plane*. The three axes are labeled "x," "y," and "z," where the z axis is parallel to the *detector axis* and the x axis and the y axis are in the *detector plane*. The orientation of the test objects and the direction of the magnetic field is referenced to the *measurement coordinate system*. See figure 3.

1.2.11 Measurement Plane

An imaginary two-dimensional surface over which the hand-held metal detectors are tested. There may be more than one *measurement plane*. The *measurement plane*(s) is (are) referenced from the *detector plane*. See figure 4.

1.2.11.1 Large Object Size Measurement Plane

The *measurement plane* at a *test separation distance* of 15 cm from the *detector plane*.

1.2.11.2 Medium Object Size Measurement Plane

The *measurement plane* at a *test separation distance* of 7.5 cm from the *detector plane*.

1.2.11.3 Small Object Size Measurement Plane

The *measurement plane* at a *test separation distance* of 5 cm from the *detector plane*.

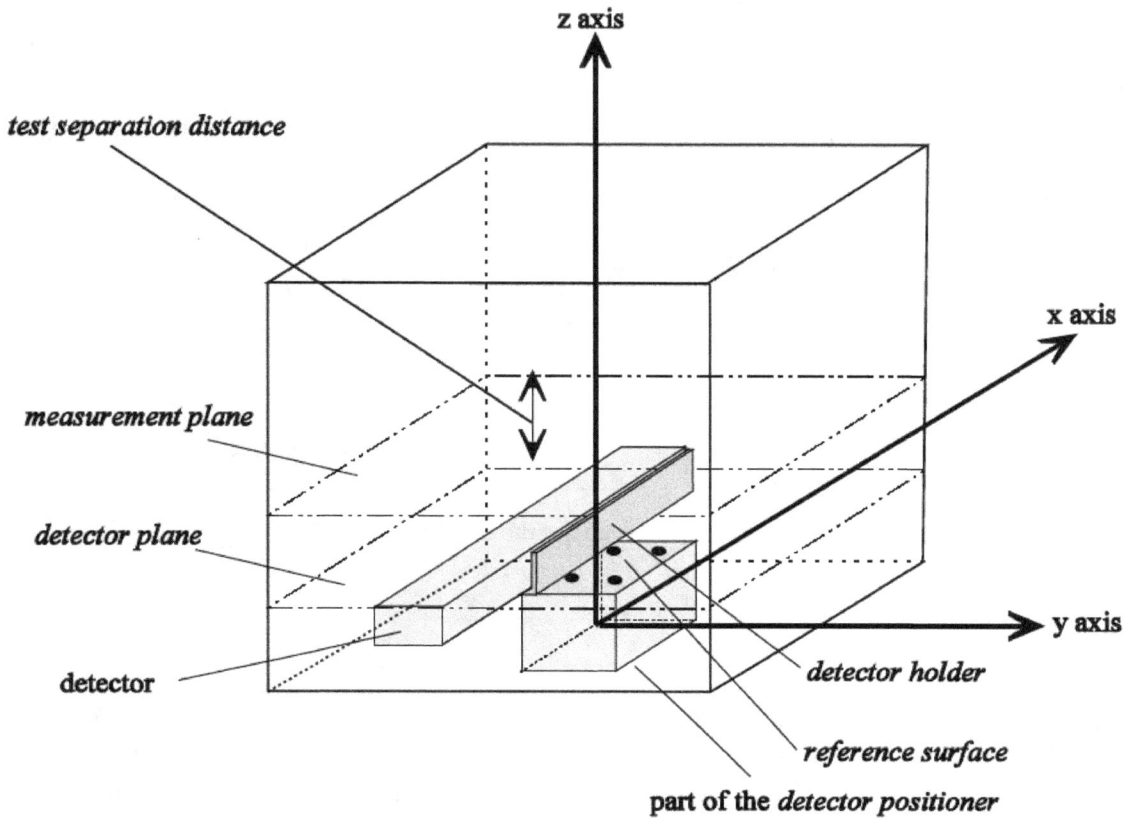

Figure 3. Diagram of the measurement coordinate system *showing the* measurement coordinate system *axes, one* measurement plane, *the* detector plane, *and the* reference surface, *where the* detector holder, *containing a detector, is unmounted*

1.2.11.4 Very Small Object Size Measurement Plane

The *measurement plane* at a *test separation distance* of 3 cm from the *detector plane.*

1.2.12 Reference Axis

An imaginary line that is perpendicular to and centered in the *reference surface.* See figure 4.

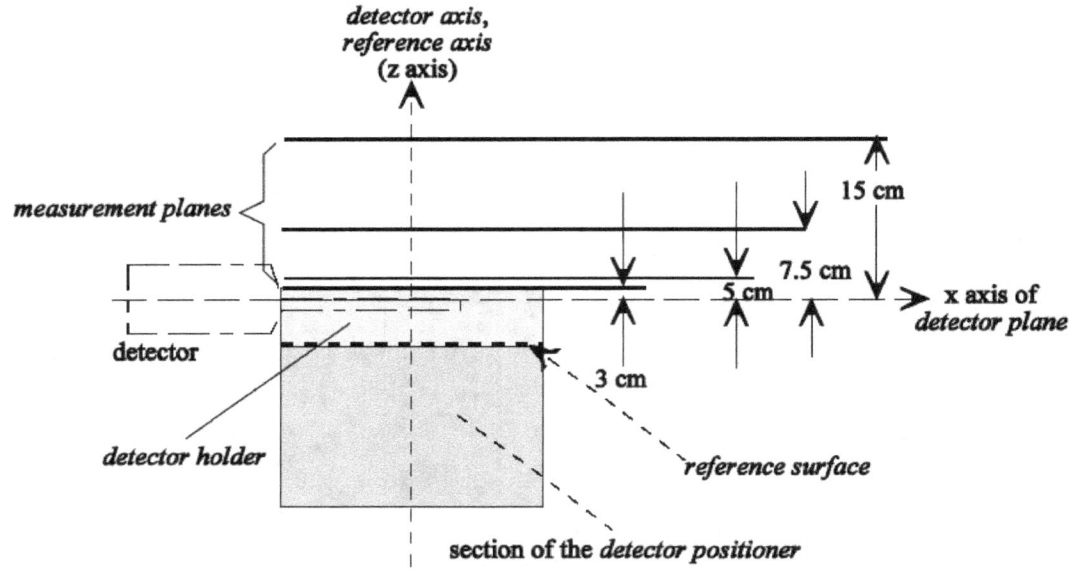

Figure 4. A schematic of the detector and the detector positioner, *with detector in place, where the* detector holder *is properly located on the* detector positioner; *that is, where the z axis of the* measurement coordinate system, *the detector axis, and the* reference axis *are collinear; the* detector holder *and* detector positioner *are in contact at their* reference surfaces; *and the long axis of the detector is collinear with the x axis of the* measurement coordinate system

1.2.13 Reference Surface

The planes located on the *detector holder* and *detector positioner* that are used to attach the *detector holder* and *detector positioner*. See figure 2.

1.2.14 Object Size Classes

A classification method based on the ability to detect metal objects of a minimum size. A detector may meet the requirements for one or all *object size classes*, as defined below.

6

1.2.14.1 Large Object Size

The ability to detect handguns concealed on an individual that are constructed of either ferromagnetic or nonferromagnetic metal.

1.2.14.2 Medium Object Size

The ability to detect knives concealed on an individual that are constructed of either ferromagnetic or nonferromagnetic metal. Knives are defined for this purpose as having blade lengths exceeding 7.5 cm (3 in).

1.2.14.3 Small Object Size

The ability to detect small weapons and contraband items concealed on an individual that are constructed of either ferromagnetic or nonferromagnetic metal. Small weapons and contraband items are defined as items that can be used to injure another person or to defeat security devices.

1.2.14.4 Very Small Object Size

The ability to detect very small hard-to-find items that are concealed on an individual and considered a threat to officer and prisoner safety or that can be used to defeat security measures. These objects are constructed of either ferromagnetic or nonferromagnetic metal.

1.2.15 Test Object

An item that is used to test the hand-held detection performance. The *test object* is an encased replica of a metallic item. This item is either a weapon, can be used as a weapon, or can be used to defeat security devices. The shape of the encasement is a parallelepiped. The encasement has up to nine orientation holes that allow the replica to be oriented with respect to the *measurement coordinate system*. These nine orientation holes are distributed on no more than three surfaces of the *test object*. Each of these surfaces has no more than three orientation holes, and one of the orientation holes is used as a center of rotation.

1.2.15.1 Large Object Size Test Objects

Test objects that are used to test the *large object size* detection performance of hand-held metal detectors used as weapon detectors. Mechanical drawings of *large object size test objects* are provided in section 5.1.

1.2.15.2 Medium Object Size Test Objects

Test objects that are used to test the *medium object size* detection performance of hand-held metal detectors used as weapon detectors. Mechanical drawings of *medium object size test objects* are provided in section 5.2.

1.2.15.3 Small Object Size Test Objects

Test objects that are used to test the *small object size* detection performance of hand-held metal detectors used as weapon detectors. Mechanical drawings of the *small object size test objects* are provided in section 5.3.

1.2.15.4 Very Small Object Size Test Objects

Test objects that are used to test the *very small object size* detection performance of hand-held metal detectors used as weapon detectors. Mechanical drawings of the *very small object size test objects* are provided in section 5.4.

1.2.16 Test Object Axes

The three mutually orthogonal axes of the *test object* that are referenced to and have a one-to-one correspondence with the axes of the *measurement coordinate system*.

1.2.17 Test Separation Distance

The distance between the *measurement plane*(s) and the *detector plane* or as otherwise specified. The *test separation distances* are 3 cm, 5 cm, 7.5 cm, and 15 cm. See figure 4.

1.2.18 Three-Axes Positioning System

Also known as a Cartesian robot, the *three-axes positioning system* provides three mutually orthogonal directions of linear translation. The *three-axes positioning system* is used to place the *test objects* in the magnetic field of the detector.

2. REQUIREMENTS FOR ACCEPTANCE

The detector shall meet the requirements and specifications stated in this section. Reports shall be provided on the Compliance Test Report forms mentioned in section 6.

2.1 Safety Specifications and Requirements

2.1.1 Electrical

The detector shall comply with UL 60950, *Safety for Information Technology Equipment*, if the potential difference between any two points within the detector is greater than 30 V rms (42.4 V peak-to-peak) for alternating currents (ac) or greater than 60 V referenced to ground for direct currents (dc).

2.1.2 Mechanical

The detector shall not expose (1) any sharp corners or edges that can puncture, cut, or tear the skin or clothing or injure persons coming in contact with the detector; (2) external wires and cables; or (3) loose covers and cowlings. The minimum exposed radius of curvature for corners and edges shall be 1 mm (0.04 in).

2.1.3 Exposure

The level of the electromagnetic field generated by the detector shall be less than the exposure limits specified in IEEE C95.1 1991, as amended.

2.1.4 Personal Medical Electronic Devices

The magnetic fields produced by the detector shall not generate voltages across the leads of the test probe specified in *Safety Code, Recommended Safety Procedures for the Selection, Installation and Use of Active Metal Detectors*, Radiation Protection Bureau, Canadian Minister of National Health and Welfare (the Code) that exceed the maximum permitted probe output specified in the Code when tested in accordance with the Code.

2.2 Electrical Requirements

2.2.1 Battery Condition

The manufacturer shall provide a visual or audible indicator to alert the operator of the battery condition as described in section 2.6.3.

2.2.2 Minimum Battery Life

The detector must be designed so that the battery life is at least 40 h as tested in accordance with section 3.5.

2.3 Detection Performance Specifications

The detection performance specifications shall be tested using the detection sensitivity setting that is specified by the manufacturer to be appropriate for each *object size class* of the detector that is to be tested. The detector need only to qualify for the smallest *object size class* specified by the manufacturer; qualification to larger *object size classes* will be assumed.

2.3.1 Detection Sensitivity

The detector shall alarm for each *test object* of the appropriate *object size class* positioned in the appropriate *measurement plane* for each allowed orientation of the *test object axes* with respect to the *measurement coordinate system* for the *test object* moving at a speed of 1.0 m/s ± 0.05 m/s and as tested in accordance with section 3.2.3. (The appropriate *measurement planes* are the *large object size, medium object size, small object size,* and *very small object size measurement planes* as defined in sec. 1.2.11).

2.3.2 Speed

The detector shall provide a *positive alarm indication* for each *test object* of the appropriate *object size class* positioned in the appropriate *measurement plane* for each allowed orientation of the *test object axes* with respect to the *measurement coordinate system* for the *test object* moving at the following speeds: 0.05 m/s ± 0.01 m/s, 0.5 m/s ± 0.01 m/s, 1.0 m/s ± 0.01 m/s, and 2.0 m/s ± 0.01 m/s as tested in accordance with section 3.2.4, and the results shall be recorded.

2.3.3 Repeatability

The detector shall provide a *positive alarm indication* without failure for each *test object* of the appropriate *object size class* positioned in the appropriate *measurement plane* for each allowed orientation of the *test object axes* with respect to the *measurement coordinate system* for the *test object* moving at a speed of 1.0 m/s ± 0.05 m/s for 50 consecutive trials under the following conditions:

a. The delay between subsequent trials of a given *test object* shall be no more than 10 s.
b. The detector sensitivity shall not be readjusted between trials of a given *test object* or between trials of the *test objects* of a given *object size class.*

The repeatability test shall be performed in accordance with section 3.2.4, and the results shall be recorded. The results of this test can also be called the probability of detection, p_d, with a required p_d of 1.00 (or 100 %).

2.4 Operating Requirements

2.4.1 Operator Controls

Only those controls indicated here shall be accessible by the operator. Other controls and adjustments that affect the detector performance shall be inaccessible to the operator.

2.4.1.1 Detector Sensitivity Programming (Optional)

If provided, the detector sensitivity shall be controlled by a discretely adjustable switch. The switch shall be located such that it is readily accessible by the operator or, upon request, to be within an enclosed area and inaccessible to the operator.

2.4.1.2 Power On/Off Switch

The detector shall have a power on/off switch.

2.4.1.3 Audible Alarm On/Off Switch

The detector shall have a means for selectively disabling the audible alarm.

2.4.2 Background Null/Automatic Adjust Feature On/Off Switch

If any feature exists on the detector to automatically adjust for or null the detection signal caused by a large metal background, the detector shall have an on/off switch for this feature.

2.4.3 Interference

2.4.3.1 Electromagnetic

2.4.3.1.1 Emission

The detector, when adjusted to meet the requirements of section 2.3.3, shall meet the requirements of EN 50081 1, as amended, if applicable.

2.4.3.1.2 Susceptibility/Immunity

2.4.3.1.2.1 General Immunity Requirements

The detector, when adjusted to meet the requirements of section 2.3.3, shall not provide a *positive alarm indication* when tested in accordance with EN 50082 1, as amended, if applicable.

2.4.3.1.2.2 Radiated Magnetic Field

The detector, when adjusted to meet the requirements of section 2.3.3, shall not provide a *positive alarm indication* when tested in accordance with MIL STD 461E, Method RS101, as amended, to the limits for Navy applications.

2.4.3.2 Metal

The detector shall not produce a *positive alarm indication* when operated near metal walls, as tested in accordance with section 3.4, but shall produce a *positive alarm indication* for each appropriate *test object* of the appropriate *object size class* positioned in the appropriate *measurement plane* for each allowed orientation of the *test object axes* with respect to the *measurement coordinate system* for the *test object* moving at a speed of 1.0 m/s ± 0.05 m/s as tested according to section 3.2.4.

2.4.3.3 Body

The detector shall not produce a *positive alarm indication* when operated at a distance from the body equal to the appropriate *test separation distance,* as tested in accordance with section 3.2.5, but shall produce a *positive alarm indication* for each *test object* of the appropriate *object size class* positioned in the appropriate *measurement plane* for each allowed orientation of the *test object axes* with respect to the *measurement coordinate system* for the *test object* moving at a speed of 1.0 m/s ± 0.05 m/s as tested according to section 3.2.4. The *test separation distances* shall be 15 cm for *test objects* of the *large object size* class, 7.5 cm for *test objects* of the *medium object size* class, 5 cm for *test objects* of the *small object size* class, and 3 cm for *test objects* of the *very small object size* class.

2.4.4 Environmental Ranges and Conditions

The detector or all of its components and their interconnections shall meet all of the requirements listed in this section. The requirements of section 2.1 and section 2.5 shall not be affected by the tests described in this section. The requirements given in this section shall be applied appropriately for either indoor or indoor/outdoor detector models. The requirements of this section shall be exhibited by no less than the first production unit for each unique detector model and for any physical modifications to that model. The tests listed in section 2.4.4 shall be performed on the same unit. The detector, if tested for any of the tests listed in section 2.4.4, shall exhibit no observable changes in the detection performance specification given in section 2.3.3.

2.4.4.1 Temperature Stability and Range

2.4.4.1.1 Indoor

The detector shall operate over the ambient temperature range of at least 0 °C to 46 °C (32 °F to 115 °F). The detector shall be tested in accordance with MIL STD 810F Method 501.4, Procedure II, at 46 °C ± 3 °C after being exposed to that temperature continuously for 24 h ± 1 h. The detector then shall be cooled to 0 °C ± 3 °C within 4 h ± 0.5 h and tested in accordance with MIL STD 810F Method 502.4, Procedure II, at 0 °C ± 3 °C after being exposed to that temperature continuously for 24 h ± 1 h.

2.4.4.1.2 Indoor/Outdoor

The detector shall operate over the ambient temperature range of at least -37 °C to 65 °C (-35 °F to 149 °F). The detector shall be tested in accordance with MIL STD 810F Method 501.4, Procedure II, at 65 °C ± 3 °C after being exposed to that temperature continuously for 24 h ± 1 h. The detector then shall be cooled to -37 °C ± 3 °C within 4 h ± 0.5 h and tested in accordance with MIL STD 810F Method 502.4, Procedure II, at -37 °C ± 3 °C after being exposed to that temperature continuously for 24 h ± 1 h.

2.4.4.2 Relative Humidity Stability and Range

The detector shall be tested in accordance with the requirements of MIL STD 810F Method 507.4, as amended.

2.4.4.3 Salt Fog, Indoor/Outdoor Only

The detector shall be tested in accordance with the requirements of MIL STD 810F Method 509.4, as amended.

2.4.4.4 Environmental Protection

The detector shall meet or exceed the requirements for compliance with IEC 60529 classification IP54.

2.4.4.5 Solar Radiation (Sunshine), Indoor/Outdoor Only

The detector shall be tested in accordance with and meet the requirements of MIL STD 810F Method 505.4, Procedure 1, as amended.

2.5 Mechanical Specifications and Requirements

2.5.1 Dimensions and Weight

The detector should be capable of being gripped by a single hand, shall weigh less than 1 kg (2.2 lb), and be designed to reduce operator fatigue during long-term use.

2.5.2 Durability/Ruggedness

The detector or all of its components and their interconnections shall meet the requirements of the following standards. The requirements of section 2.1 and section 2.4 shall not be affected by the tests described in this section. All tests listed in section 2.5.2 shall be performed on the same unit. The detector, if tested for any of the tests listed in section 2.5.2.1, shall exhibit no observable changes in the detection performance specification given in section 2.3.3.

2.5.2.1 Shock

The detector shall be tested in accordance with the requirements of IEC 68 2 27 1987, as amended, using the half-sine pulse shape with a nominal peak acceleration of 30 g (300 m/s^2) and a nominal pulse duration of 6 ms.

2.5.2.2 Bump

The detector shall be tested in accordance with the requirements of IEC 68 2 29 1987, as amended, using 100 bumps each with a nominal peak acceleration of 40 g (400 m/s^2) and a nominal pulse duration of 6 ms.

2.5.2.3 Free Fall

The detector shall be tested in accordance with the requirements of IEC 68 2 32 Procedure 1, 1975, as amended, for each direction of the *detector axes* and a fall height of 1 m.

2.5.2.4 Pressure Resistance

The detector shall be capable of withstanding the force of 600 N (135 lb) over any 1 cm x 1 cm (0.4 in x 0.4 in) area on the detector for a sustained period of 1 min.

2.6 Functional Requirements

2.6.1 Audible Alarms

All audible indicators (other than an earphone) shall produce an alarm-state sound pressure level 0.8 m $\pm$ 0.08 m from the detector of 85 dB_{SPL} $\pm$ 5 dB_{SPL} measured in accordance with section 3.3.2. For status indicators, the audible alarm shall be a two-state audible alarm: active (alarm state) and inactive (nonalarm state). For metal object warning, the audible alarm shall be a frequency-proportional audible alarm or, optionally, a two-state audible alarm.

2.6.1.1 Earphone Jack (Optional)

If an earphone jack is supplied with the hand-held metal detector, the earphone shall disable the audible *alarm indicator* when the earphone is plugged into the earphone jack.

2.6.1.2 Alarm Indicator for Metal Object Detection

The detector shall have either a frequency-proportional *alarm indicator* (see sec. 2.6.1.2.1) or a two-state *alarm indicator* (see sec. 2.6.1.2.2).

2.6.1.2.1 Frequency-Proportional Alarm Indicator for Metal Object Detection

The frequency-proportional *alarm indicator* shall provide an audible *alarm indication* with an audio frequency output that is continuously proportional to the detection signal. The frequency-proportional *alarm indication* shall have a quiescent state frequency drift rate, measured in accordance with section 3.3.3, of not more than 5 Hz/s. The *proportional alarm indication* shall vary by at least 2000 Hz within the frequency range of 500 Hz to 4000 Hz for objects varying in size from the smallest *test objects* of the appropriate *object size class* to the metal test panel described in section 3.4.1.

2.6.1.2.2 Two-State Alarm Indicator for Metal Object Detection

The two-state *alarm indicator* shall provide a two-state audible *alarm indication* to alert the operator about the presence of a metal object. The two-state alarm indicator shall produce no sound in the nonalarm state and shall produce an audio frequency alarm within the range of 500 Hz to 4000 Hz with a -3 dB frequency bandwidth of less than 1 % of the selected operating frequency and a frequency drift of less than 5 Hz/s and less than 1 % of the selected operating frequency over any 2-h period.

2.6.2 Visual Indicators

Any visible *alarm indication* shall be readily perceptible when tested in accordance with section 3.3.4. The visual *alarm indicators* shall be a two-state visual alarm: active (illuminating) and inactive (nonilluminating).

2.6.2.1 Metal Object Detection

The detector shall have a visual alarm indicating the presence of a metal object in the *target space*. The alarm state for the metal-object-detection visual *alarm indicator* shall be active (illuminating), and the nonalarm state shall be inactive (nonilluminating). The metal-object-detection visual *alarm indicator* shall be distinct from any other visual *alarm indicators*.

2.6.3 Battery Condition Indicator

The detector shall have a visual or audible alarm indicating the condition of the battery and shall be activated if the battery condition drops to a level that can cause a degradation of the detection performance required by this standard.

2.6.4 Interchangeability

Any model detector manufactured by the same manufacturer shall be compatible with previous revisions of the same model (backwardly compatible). In particular, the components shall be backwardly compatible.

2.7 Detector Holder

The manufacturer shall provide with each detector, if requested, a holder for mounting the detector on the *reference surface* (see fig. 5) of the measurement system (see figs. 2 and 3). The *detector holder* shall comply with section 2.1.2 and shall meet the following specifications:

a. Relative permeability 1.0 ± 0.001.
b. Electrical conductivity $< 10^{-8}$ Siemens/m.
c. Mass ≤ 2 kg (4.5 lb).
d. Surface flatness ± 0.5 mm (0.041 in).
e. Firmly holds the detector.
f. Mates with the *reference surface*.
g. Fastener holes align with each of the four 1/4-20 fastener holes of the *reference surface* (see figs. 2, 3, and 5).
h. Holds the detector so that the *detector axis* and *reference axis* are collinear.
i. Holds the detector so that the longest axis of the detector that is parallel to the *detector plane* is collinear with the x axis of the *measurement coordinate system*.

j. Holds the detector so that the *detector plane* is 10 cm ± 0.1 cm from the *reference surface*.

k. The top surface should be located less than 2.5 cm from the *detector plane*. If the detector is of such shape and geometry that access to the *measurement plane* at a *test separation distance* of 2.5 cm is not possible, then the *test separation distance* for the closest possible *measurement plane* shall be reported.

l. Holds the detector such that no part of the detector is above the *measurement plane* at a *test separation distance* of 2.5 cm.

2.8 Quality Control and Assurance

2.8.1 Quality Systems

The manufacturer shall meet the requirements of ISO 9001:2000, as amended.

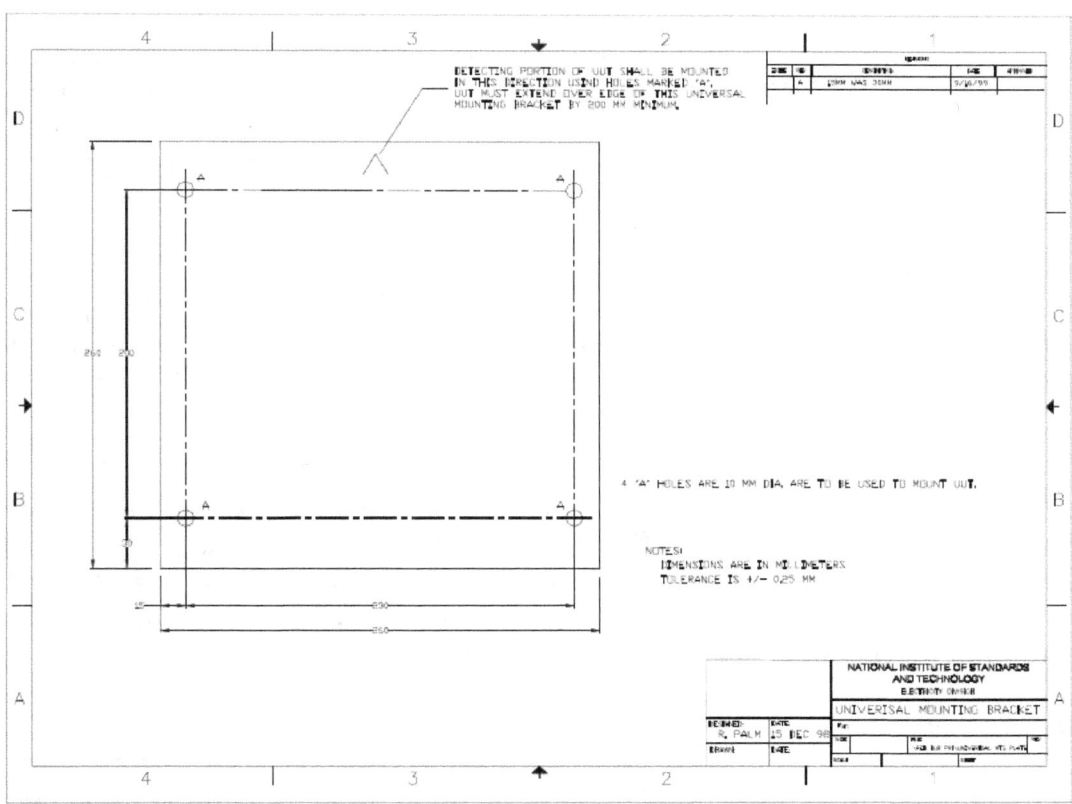

Figure 5. Mechanical drawing of the reference surface

17

2.8.2 Testing and Calibration Laboratories

Laboratories performing testing and calibration of the detector and/or its components shall meet the requirements of ISO 17025, as amended.

2.8.3 Measurement Equipment and Processes

All measurement equipment and processes shall meet the requirements of ISO 10012 1, as amended, and ISO 10012 2, as amended.

2.8.4 Burn-In

Power-on dynamic burn-in testing for a set of metal detectors of the same model is required in accordance with section 3.6. The set shall consist of m detectors of the same type and model selected using simple random sampling methods and tested without replacement where
$m = \dfrac{0.1\,Mk_M}{0.1\,k_M + 0.01\,M}$. M is the number of the manufactured detectors of the same model, and k_M is the coverage factor for the 99 % confidence interval. (See table B.1 of B.N. Taylor and C.E. Kuyatt, NIST Technical Note 1297, *Guidelines for Evaluating and Expressing the Uncertainty of NIST Measurement Results,* U.S. Government Printing Office, Washington, DC, 1994.) The manufacturer shall provide the test results of this randomly selected set of the same type and model detectors.

2.8.5 Power Cycling

Power cycling testing for a set of metal detectors of the same model is required in accordance with section 3.7. The set shall consist of m detectors of the same type and model selected using simple random sampling methods and tested without replacement where $m = \dfrac{0.1\,Mk_M}{0.1\,k_M + 0.01\,M}$. M is the number of the manufactured detectors of the same model and k_M is the coverage factor for the 99 % confidence interval. (See Table B.1 of B.N. Taylor and C.E. Kuyatt, NIST Technical Note 1297, *Guidelines for Evaluating and Expressing the Uncertainty of NIST Measurement Results,* U.S. Government Printing Office, Washington, DC, 1994.) The manufacturer shall provide the test results of this randomly selected set of the same type and model detectors.

2.9 Documentation

The manufacturer shall provide the following list of deliverable items with each detector unless otherwise indicated.

2.9.1 Operating Instructions

An operator's manual shall be supplied by the manufacturer or distributor with each detector and shall contain at least the following information:

a. The purpose of the detector.
b. A description of operator controls.
c. A list of operating features.
d. A description of detection principles and detector capabilities.
e. A block diagram showing the major internal functional components.
f. An exposure warning that states, "This Device May Affect Personal Medical Electronic Devices" until such time that the Food and Drug Administration or some other competent Federal agency requires a different warning or has determined that no such warning is necessary.

2.9.2 Operator Training Instructions and Videotape or CD–ROM

A training package shall be supplied upon request that will provide operators with the information necessary to acquire the technical and operational skills required to conduct effective screening with the detector. The training package shall include an audio/visual videotape or CD ROM and an operator's manual. For additional guidance in formulating the operator training package, review *A Users' Guide for Hand-Held and Walk-Through Metal Weapon Detectors* (National Institute of Justice, NIJ Guide 600 00, 2001). The manufacturer shall have demonstrated the effectiveness of the training material when 50 % of the test group receiving the training understands the operation of the detector, passes a written test, and operates the detector successfully. The test group shall consist of at least 10 people with only a high school education.

2.9.3 Technical Manual

A technical manual that contains all of the information that could be required by a technician to troubleshoot, maintain, and repair the equipment to the component level shall be provided upon request.

2.9.4 Technical Training Manual and Videotape or CD–ROM

A self-study training package shall be provided upon request for use by site maintenance technicians. The training package must consist of an audio/visual videotape or CD ROM and a technical manual that provides detailed explanations of circuit theory and maintenance procedures.

2.9.5 Technical Specifications

The manufacturer shall provide, upon request, a detailed listing of all relevant specifications of the detector. This list shall include at a minimum:

a. Detector *object size class* (as defined in sec. 1.2.14).
b. Mechanical drawings of the detector with dimensions in metric units.
c. Mass of the detector.
d. Allowable range of ac line power supply voltage.
e. Battery type, quantity, and life.
f. Maximum magnetic field strength that can be found on the detector surface.
g. If applicable, operating frequency and, if applicable, modulation parameters.
h. If applicable, pulse repetition rate, pulse duration, and pulse transition duration.
i. Operating ambient temperature range.

2.9.6 Certification of Test, Inspection, and Conformance

The manufacturer shall provide, upon request, a certification of all mandatory tests; test procedures; testing laboratories; compliance to required standards; a record of the test results for the detector; and the identities of all the companies, laboratories, and/or organizations conducting the tests.

2.9.7 Suggested Maintenance Schedule

The manufacturer shall provide a preventive maintenance schedule and a detailed list of the technical skills, computer hardware, and software tools required.

2.9.8 Installation Instructions

The manufacturer shall provide instructions for battery installation and specify the type and quantity of batteries required.

3. PERFORMANCE TESTING PROCEDURES

The detector shall meet the detection performance requirements for each *object size class* in which it is required to operate. The detection performance shall be evaluated by the test methods described in this section. The manufacturer shall record and provide the test results on the report forms mentioned in section 6 of this randomly selected set of same type and model detectors.

3.1 General Test Conditions

3.1.1 Test Location

The distance between any metal object other than a *test object* and the closest part of the detector shall be greater than 0.8 m (31 in).

3.1.2 Environment

At the time of the tests, the ambient temperature shall be in the range specified in section 2.4.4.1 for the appropriate application (indoor or indoor/outdoor); the relative humidity shall be noncondensing.

3.1.3 Preparations

New batteries of the type listed in the operator's manual shall be installed at the beginning of the tests and as instructed in any test method. Any setup or calibration adjustments specified in the operator's manual shall be performed if required.

3.2 Detection Performance Tests

3.2.1 Object Size Classes

If the detector can be adjusted to provide an *alarm indication* for more than one *object size class*, the detection performance test shall be performed for each *object size class*. The detection performance shall be evaluated by the test methods described in this section. The distinction in testing between the different *object size classes* is the difference in the *test separation distance* of the *measurement plane* and the *test objects*.

3.2.2 Equipment

3.2.2.1 Test Objects

Test objects shall be as described in section 5. There are up to three orientation holes on up to three surfaces of the *test object* (encased replica of a threat item). The tapped hole on each surface of the *test objects* is labeled with an "A" (see mechanical drawings in sec. 5 showing the encased *test object*) and is the center of rotation of the different orientations. The *test objects* shall be oriented such that the orienting holes being used are facing the *three-axes positioning system* as the *test objects* pass by the detector and that the hole labeled "A" is below the other orientation hole being used. The *measurement plane* shall pass through the *test object* at the point labeled "A" and be parallel to the bottom surface of the *test object*. If the detector is of such shape and geometry that access to the *measurement plane* at a *test separation distance* of 3 cm is not possible, then the *test separation distance* for the closest possible *measurement plane* shall be reported. Labeling for the *test object* orientation shall use two characters: the first character indicates in which quadrant of the mechanical drawing the specified orientation can be found, and the second character indicates the position of the unused hole relative to the hole labeled "A." The quadrant designations are given as follows:

a. "1" indicates bottom left.
b. "2" indicates bottom right.
c. "3" indicates top left.
d. "4" indicates top right.

Not all quadrants are used. For the second character, "L" indicates that the unused hole is to the left of the hole labeled "A," and "R" indicates that the unused hole is to the right of the hole labeled "A."

3.2.2.2 Three-Axes Positioning System

The *three-axes positioning system* shall meet the following requirements:

a. Displacement, x and y axes: ≥ 1 m.
b. Displacement, z axis: ≥ 2 m.
c. Position accuracy, each axis: 1 mm.
d. Position repeatability, each axis: 1 mm.
e. Maximum slew speed, y axis: ≥ 2 m/s.

3.2.2.3 Microphone (Audible *Alarm Indicators*)

The microphone is the audible *alarm indication* detector. It shall be used to detect an audible *positive alarm indication,* be capable of detecting the audible *alarm indication* as described in section 2.6.1, and provide an analog output that can be interfaced to the computer controller (see sec. 3.2.2.6).

3.2.2.4 Light Detector (Visible *Alarm Indicators*)

The light detector is the visible *alarm indication* detector. It shall be used to detect a visible *positive alarm indication,* be capable of being attached directly to the visual alarm indicator, and provide an analog electrical output that can be interfaced to the computer controller (see sec. 3.2.2.6).

3.2.2.5 Detector Positioner

The *detector positioner* is a nonmagnetic, nonconductive device that provides a surface on which to securely attach the *detector holder* and that places the detector at a fixed location in the *measurement coordinate system* relative to the *three-axes positioning system*. A diagram of the *detector holder* showing the *reference axis, reference surface,* and x, y, and z *measurement coordinate system* axes is given in figure 4. A detailed mechanical drawing of the *reference surface* is provided in figure 5.

3.2.2.6 Computer Controller

The computer controller shall have installed and operational all necessary hardware and software for providing instrument control and data acquisition.

3.2.3 Detection Sensitivity

3.2.3.1 Initial Procedures

Ensure that the *alarm indication* detector and positioning system are connected to the computer controller. Turn on the *alarm indication* detector, computer controller, and positioning system and verify proper operation of the measurement system. Ensure that the hand-held metal detector is securely held by the *detector holder* and fasten the *detector holder* to the *detector positioner.* Attach the *test object* with the proper orientation to the positioning system. Turn on the hand-held metal detector and ensure that its output is functioning properly by noting a change in the *alarm indication* detector output as a metal object is brought near the hand-held metal detector. Ensure that the *test object* does not hit any objects while in motion.

3.2.3.2 Performing the Measurement

Set the computer program to perform an x-y scan in the specified *measurement plane* at the specified speed. Set the x-axis position to -10 cm ± 0.1 cm relative to the *detector axis* and scan the y axis. Record any *positive alarm indication* using the *alarm indication* detector as the y-axis scan is being performed. Increment the x-axis position by 2 cm ± 0.1 cm and perform a y-axis scan. Repeat the x-axis increment and y-axis scan until the x-axis position is approximately 10 cm ± 0.1 cm. The center for the y-axis scans shall be the *detector axis,* and the scans shall each be 20 cm ± 0.1 cm long.

3.2.4 Speed

3.2.4.1 Initial Procedures

Ensure that the *alarm indication* detector and *three-axes positioning system* are connected to the computer controller. Turn on the *alarm indication* detector, computer controller, and *three-axes positioning system* and verify proper operation of the measurement system. Ensure that the hand-held metal detector is securely held by the *detector holder* and fasten the *detector holder* to the *detector positioner.* Attach the *test object* with the proper orientation to the *three-axes positioning system.* Turn on the hand-held metal detector and ensure that the detector output is functioning properly by noting a change in the *alarm indication* detector output as a metal object is brought near the hand-held metal detector. Ensure that the *test object* does not hit any objects while in motion.

3.2.4.2 Performing the Measurement

Set the computer program to perform a y-axis scan passing through the *detector axis* in the appropriate *measurement plane* at the specified speed. Record any *positive alarm indication* with the *alarm indication* detector as the y-axis scan is being performed. The center of the y-axis scan shall be the *detector axis* in the appropriate *measurement plane,* and the y-axis scan shall be 20 cm ± 0.1 cm long.

3.2.5 Body Interference

3.2.5.1 Initial Procedures

Select a person (the tester), whose hand and wrist are void of any metal objects, to hold the detector. The tester shall hold the detector such that the *detector plane* is parallel to the palm of the tester, the palm of the tester shall face the detector, and the arms of the tester shall extend fully away from the body. Turn on the *alarm indication* detector and the hand-held metal detector and ensure that the hand-held metal detector output is functioning properly by noting a change in the *alarm indication* detector output as a metal object is brought near the hand-held metal detector.

3.2.5.2 Performing the Measurement

Position the hand-held metal detector at the appropriate *test separation distance* from the palm of the tester and note any *positive alarm indication.*

3.3 Alarm Indication Tests

3.3.1 Equipment

3.3.1.1 Sound Level Meter

The sound pressure level meter shall comply with ANSI S1.4, 1971, for type 3, A-weighting, reference pressure 20 μPa.

3.3.1.2 Audio Frequency Measurement System

The system for measuring the fundamental audio frequency of an audible alarm indication shall be capable of measuring a frequency difference with an accuracy of 1 Hz and be capable of providing a new measurement within 4 s after a change in frequency.

24

3.3.1.3 Illumination Meter

The illumination meter shall be capable of measuring light levels of 25 lm/m² and 10 000 lm/m² with an error of not more than 10 %. The integrated spectral response shall be within 10 % of the Commission Internationale de l'Eclairage (CIE, the International Commission on Illumination) photopic curve.

3.3.2 Sound Pressure Level Test

Perform the test in an anechoic chamber or at an outdoor location at least 6 m from any large object, where the ambient sound pressure level at the time of the test is not more than 53 dB_{SPL}. Position the sound pressure level meter microphone 0.80 m ± 0.02 m from the detector. Measure the sound pressure level with the detector power applied and the *alarm indicator* in the nonalarm state. Then position the appropriate test object at a *test separation distance* of approximately 5 cm to produce an alarm, and again measure the sound pressure level.

3.3.3 Frequency Stability Test

After the detector has been off for at least 5 min, turn the detector on and complete any operator adjustments specified in the operator's manual within 10 s. Measure the frequency at 15 s ± 1 s and again at 45 s ± 1 s after the detector has been turned on. Compute the average frequency drift rate by taking the difference between the measured frequencies and dividing by 30 s. Perform the procedure three more times and compute the mean of the average frequency drift rates.

3.3.4 Visible Alarm Indicator Test

Position the detector with its alarm indicator 0.80 m ± 0.02 m from the eyes, at a test site where the ambient illumination is 10 000 lm/m² ± 1000 lm/m². After waiting at least 3 min to allow for eye accommodation, turn on the detector and move a metal object near the detector to cause an alarm. Observe the indication. Repeat the test at a test site where the ambient illumination is 25 lm/m² ± 2.5 lm/m².

3.4 Test for Operation Near a Metal Wall

3.4.1 Metal Test Panel

The metal test panel shall be cold-finished sheet carbon steel UNS G10150 to G10200, 1 m ± 0.1 m by 1 m ± 0.1 m by 0.75 mm ± 0.13 mm thick. The panel shall be mounted or supported in a manner that keeps the panel flat.

3.4.2 Procedure

Position the detector with its *detector plane* parallel to and 0.5 m ± 0.01 m from the plane of the test panel and with the *detector axis* centered with respect to the test panel. Turn on the detector and adjust its controls as specified in the operator's manual. Note the *alarm indicator* response.

3.5 Battery Life Test

Install in the detector new or fully charged batteries of the type specified by the manufacturer. Turn the detector on and leave it on for a continuous 40 h ± 1 h period. Within 1 h from the end of this period and without changing the batteries, test the detector in accordance with section 2.3.3 for the *test object* of the appropriate *object size class,* its material, and its orientation (see sec. 3.2.2.1) given below:

    a. *Large object size:* Handgun: material, zinc; orientation, 3L.
    b. *Medium object size:* Knife: material, aluminum; orientation, 3L.
    c. *Small object size:* Stainless steel knife: orientation, 3L.
    d. *Very small object size:* Razor blade: orientation, 3L.

3.6 Burn-In Test

Turn the detector on (such that it is ready to detect a metal object) for a period of 160 h ± 5 h. Replace the battery once every 40 h ± 1 h, if necessary. Without turning the detector off, test the detector in accordance with section 2.3.3 for the *test object* of the appropriate *object size class,* its material, and its orientation (see sec. 3.2.2.1) given below:

    a. *Large object size:* Handgun: material, zinc; orientation, 3L.
    b. *Medium object size:* Knife: material, aluminum; orientation, 3L.
    c. *Small object size:* Stainless steel knife: orientation, 3L.
    d. *Very small object size:* Razor blade: orientation, 3L.

3.7 Power Cycling Test

Turn the detector power on and off 100 times ± 2 times within 300 s ± 30 s and immediately (within 60 s) test the detector in accordance with section 2.3.3 for the *test object* of the appropriate *object size class,* its material, and its orientation (see sec. 3.2.2.1) given below:

    a. *Large object size:* Handgun: material, zinc; orientation, 3L.
    b. *Medium object size:* Knife: material, aluminum; orientation, 3L.
    c. *Small object size:* Stainless steel knife: orientation, 3L.
    d. *Very small object size:* Razor blade: orientation, 3L.

4. FIELD TESTING PROCEDURES

4.1 Large Object Size

The detector shall provide a *positive alarm indication* when passed approximately 15 cm (6 in) from the *large object size test objects* described in section 5.1. Repeat this test three times at pass-by speeds ranging from approximately 0.5 m/s to approximately 1.5 m/s to ensure proper detector performance.

4.2 Medium Object Size

The detector shall provide a *positive alarm indication* when passed approximately 7.5 cm (3 in) from the *medium object size test objects* described in section 5.2. Repeat this test three times at pass-by speeds ranging from approximately 0.5 m/s to approximately 1.5 m/s to ensure proper detector performance.

4.3 Small Object Size

The detector shall provide a *positive alarm indication* when passed approximately 5 cm (2 in) from the *small object size test objects* described in section 5.3. Repeat this test three times at pass-by speeds ranging from approximately 0.5 m/s to approximately 1.5 m/s to ensure proper detector performance.

4.4 Very Small Object Size

The detector shall provide a *positive alarm indication* when passed approximately 3 cm (1.2 in) from the *very small object size test objects* described in section 5.4. Repeat this test three times at pass-by speeds ranging from approximately 0.5 m/s to approximately 1.5 m/s to ensure proper detector performance.

5. TEST OBJECTS DESCRIPTION

This section contains mechanical drawings of the *test objects*. The *test objects* are encased replicas of threat items. All dimensions in the mechanical drawings are given in units of millimeters (mm).

5.1 Large Object Size Test Objects

The following mechanical drawings are of replicas of the *large object size* item that is considered a threat to an officer, a prisoner, an inmate, and public safety. The *large object size* threat item is a handgun. The mechanical drawings are arranged in the following order: the replica of the handgun and the location of the replica within the encasement. Three replicas are made and encased, one from each of the materials indicated in the drawings.

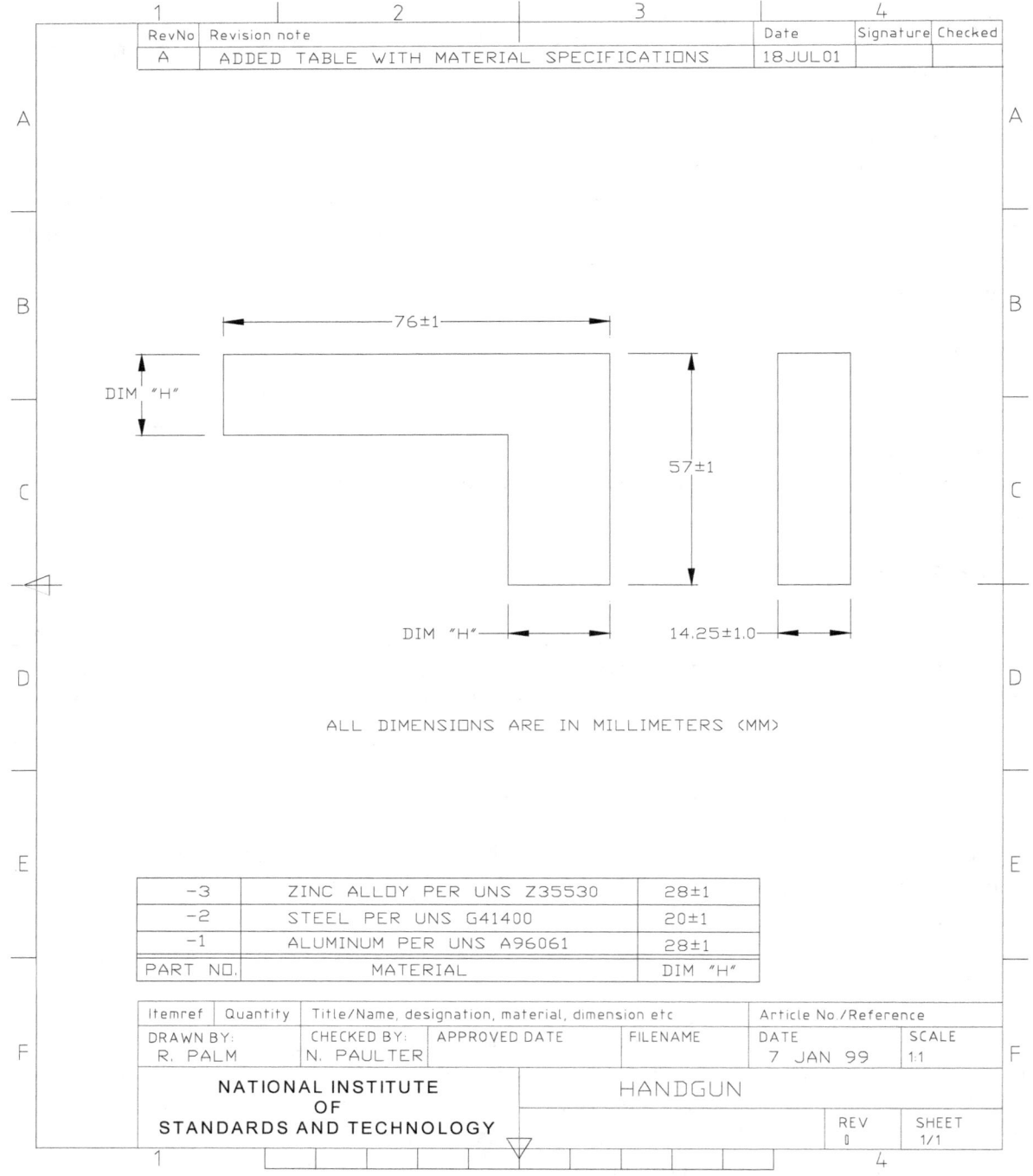

DIM "H"

76±1

57±1

DIM "H"

14.25±1.0

ALL DIMENSIONS ARE IN MILLIMETERS (MM)

PART NO.	MATERIAL	DIM "H"
−3	ZINC ALLOY PER UNS Z35530	28±1
−2	STEEL PER UNS G41400	20±1
−1	ALUMINUM PER UNS A96061	28±1

Itemref	Quantity	Title/Name, designation, material, dimension etc		Article No./Reference	
DRAWN BY: R. PALM	CHECKED BY: N. PAULTER	APPROVED DATE	FILENAME	DATE 7 JAN 99	SCALE 1:1

NATIONAL INSTITUTE OF STANDARDS AND TECHNOLOGY

HANDGUN

REV 0 · SHEET 1/1

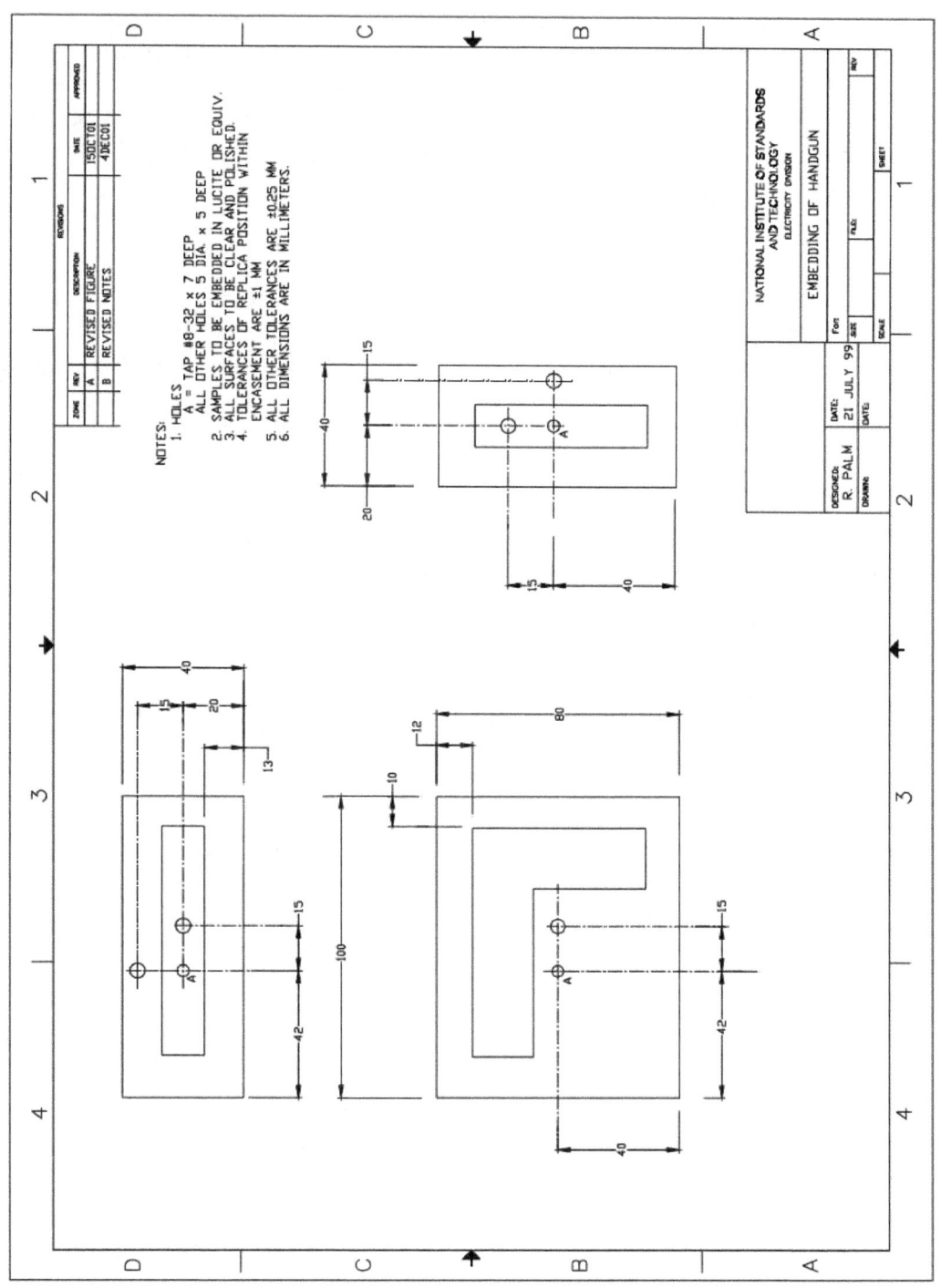

NOTES:
1. HOLES
   A = TAP #8-32 × 7 DEEP
   ALL OTHER HOLES 5 DIA. × 5 DEEP
2. SAMPLES TO BE EMBEDDED IN LUCITE OR EQUIV.
3. ALL SURFACES TO BE CLEAR AND POLISHED.
4. TOLERANCES OF REPLICA POSITION WITHIN
   ENCASEMENT ARE ±1 MM
5. ALL OTHER TOLERANCES ARE ±0.25 MM
6. ALL DIMENSIONS ARE IN MILLIMETERS.

NATIONAL INSTITUTE OF STANDARDS
AND TECHNOLOGY
ELECTRICITY DIVISION

EMBEDDING OF HANDGUN

DESIGNED: R. PALM
DATE: 21 JULY 99

5.2 Medium Object Size Test Objects

The following mechanical drawings are of the replicas of the *medium object size* item that is considered a threat to an officer, a prisoner, an inmate, and public safety. The *medium object size* threat item is a knife. The mechanical drawings are arranged in the following order: the replica of the knife and the location of the replica within the encasement. Two replicas are made and encased, one from each of the materials indicated in the drawings.

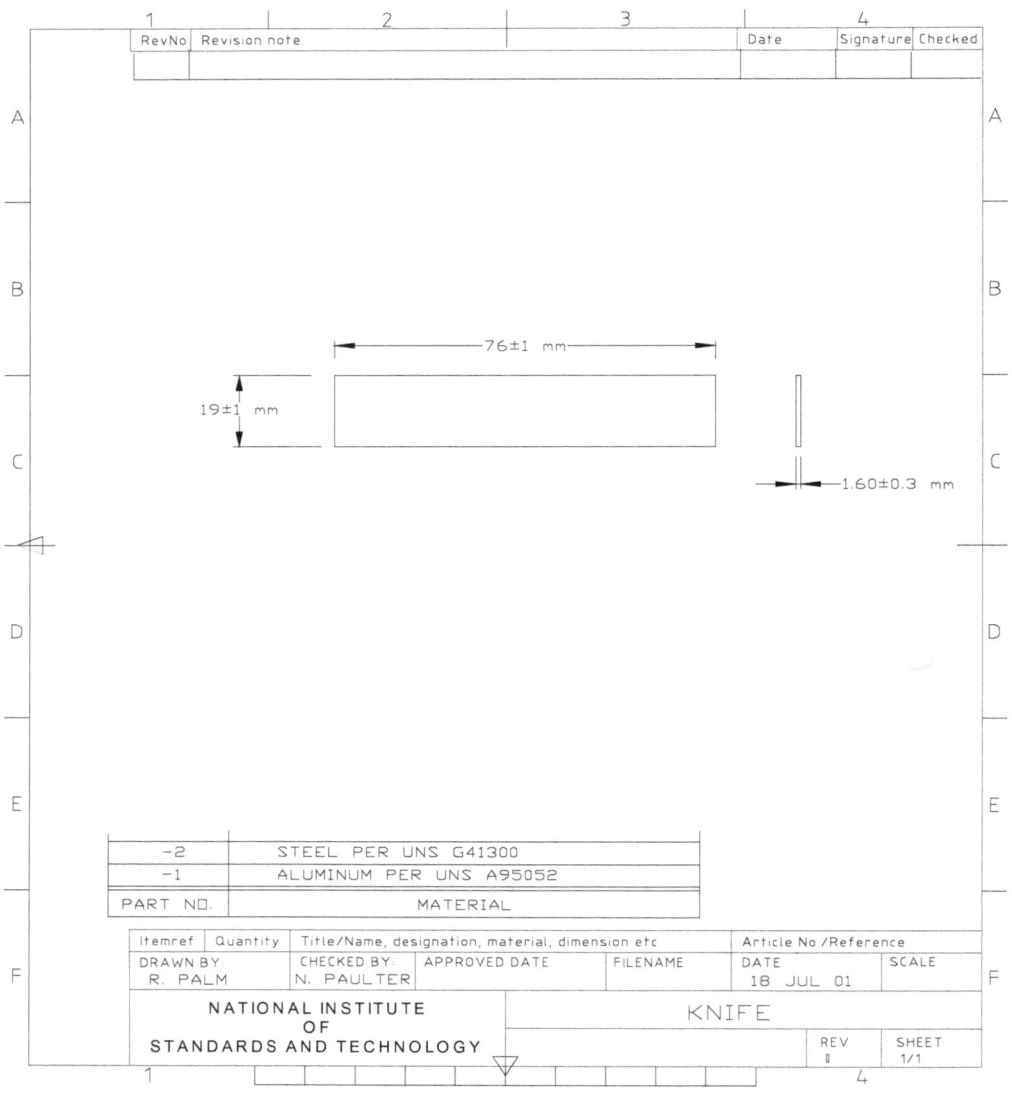

		1	2	3	4		
RevNo	Revision note				Date	Signature	Checked

76±1 mm

19±1 mm

1.60±0.3 mm

	-2	STEEL PER UNS G41300
	-1	ALUMINUM PER UNS A95052
PART NO.		MATERIAL

Itemref	Quantity	Title/Name, designation, material, dimension etc		Article No /Reference		
DRAWN BY: R. PALM	CHECKED BY: N. PAULTER	APPROVED DATE	FILENAME	DATE 18 JUL 01	SCALE	

NATIONAL INSTITUTE
OF
STANDARDS AND TECHNOLOGY

KNIFE

REV	SHEET
0	1/1

30

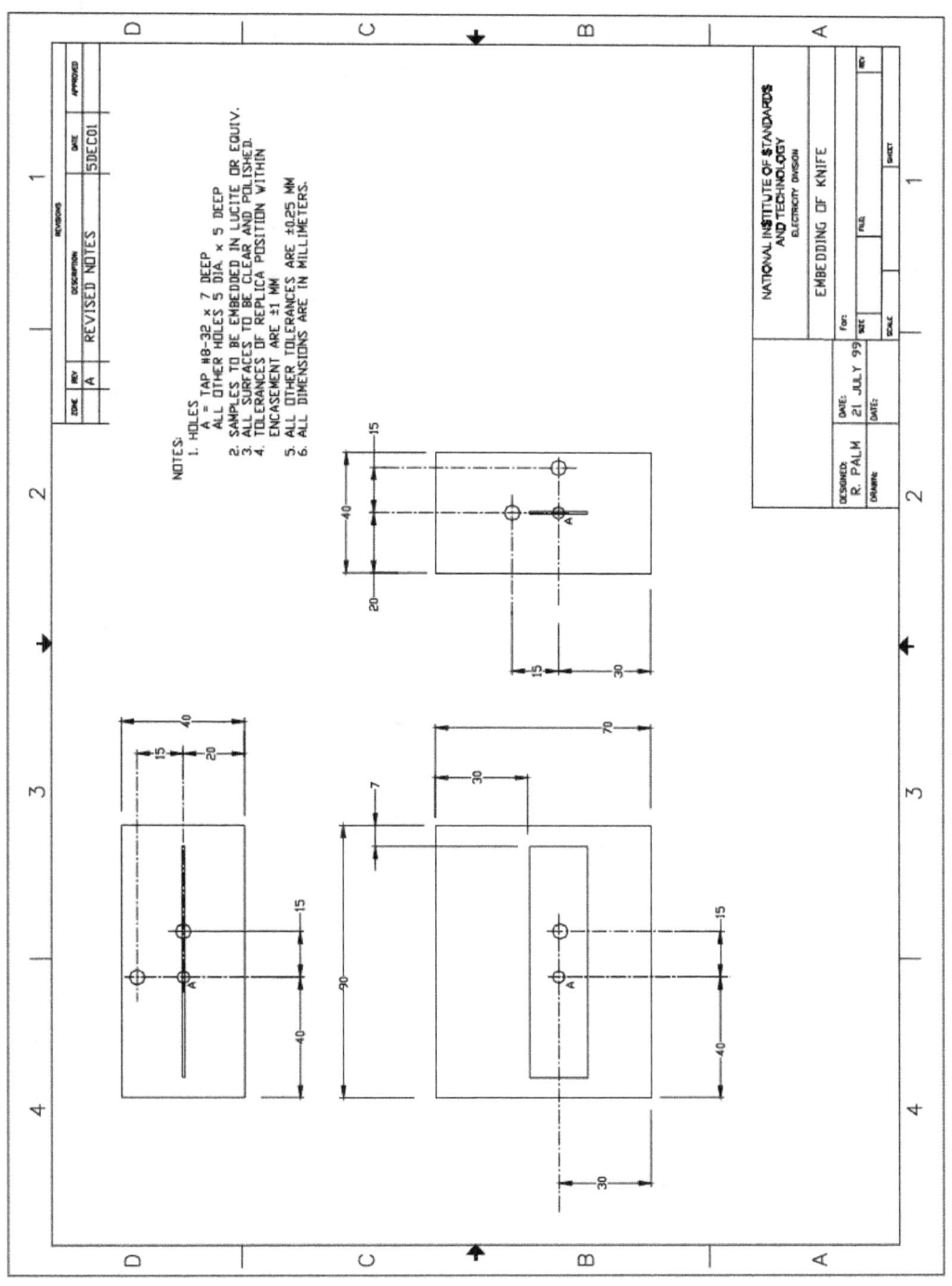

NOTES:
1. HOLES : TAP #8-32 x 7 DEEP
   A = TAP HOLES 5 DIA x 5 DEEP
   ALL OTHER HOLES 5 DIA x 5 DEEP
2. SAMPLES TO BE EMBEDDED IN LUCITE OR EQUIV.
3. ALL SURFACES TO BE CLEAR AND POLISHED.
4. TOLERANCES OF REPLICA POSITION WITHIN
   ENCASEMENT ARE ±1 MM
5. ALL OTHER TOLERANCES ARE ±0.25 MM
6. ALL DIMENSIONS ARE IN MILLIMETERS.

ZONE	REV	DESCRIPTION	DATE	APPROVED
	A	REVISED NOTES	5DEC01	

REVISIONS

NATIONAL INSTITUTE OF STANDARDS
AND TECHNOLOGY
ELECTRICITY DIVISION

EMBEDDING OF KNIFE

DESIGNED: R. PALM
DATE: 21 JULY 99

5.3 Small Object Size Test Objects

The following mechanical drawings are replicas of the *small object size* items that are considered a threat to officer and prisoner safety and that can be used to defeat security measures. These items are replicas of a handcuff key, a nonferromagnetic stainless steel knife, and a 22-caliber Long Rifle cartridge.

5.3.1 Handcuff Key

This section contains mechanical drawings of the replica of a handcuff key, a *small object size test object.* The mechanical drawings are arranged in the following order: the replica of the handcuff key and the location of the replica within the encasement.

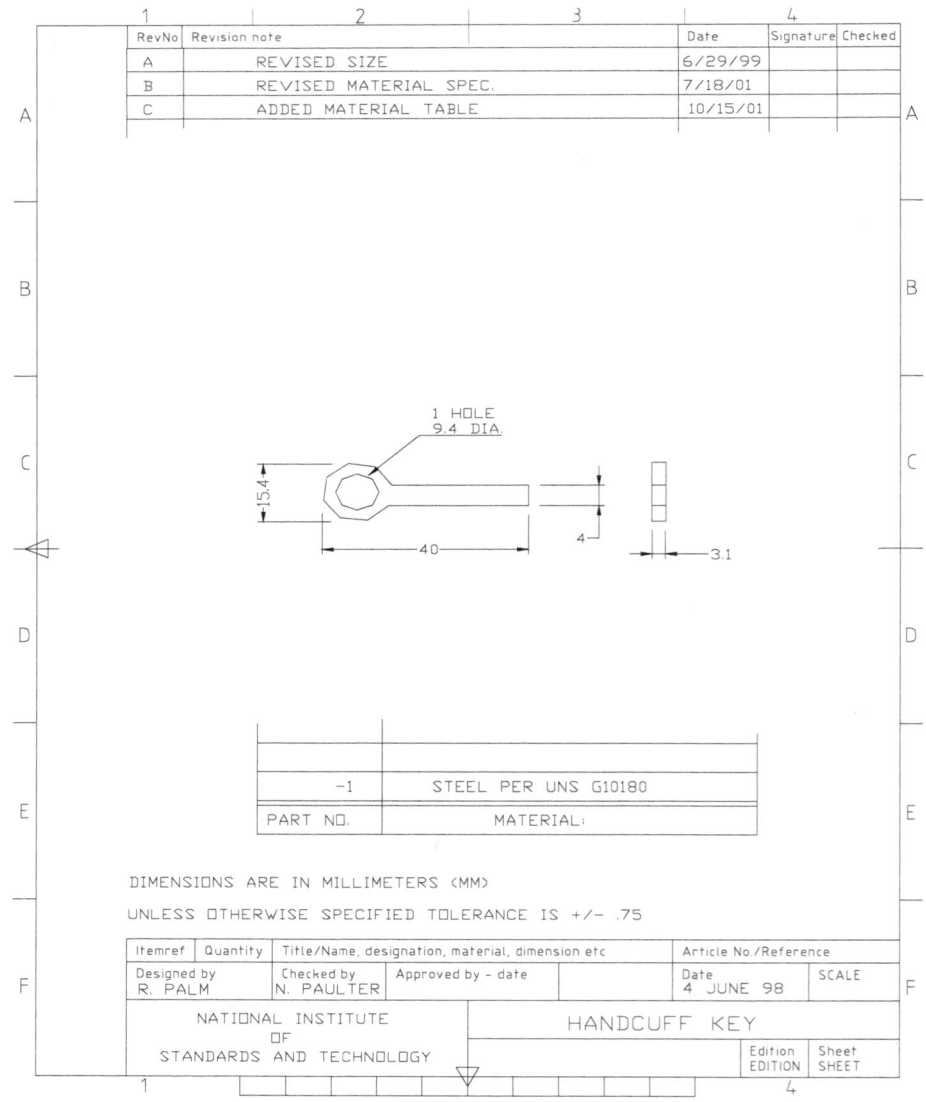

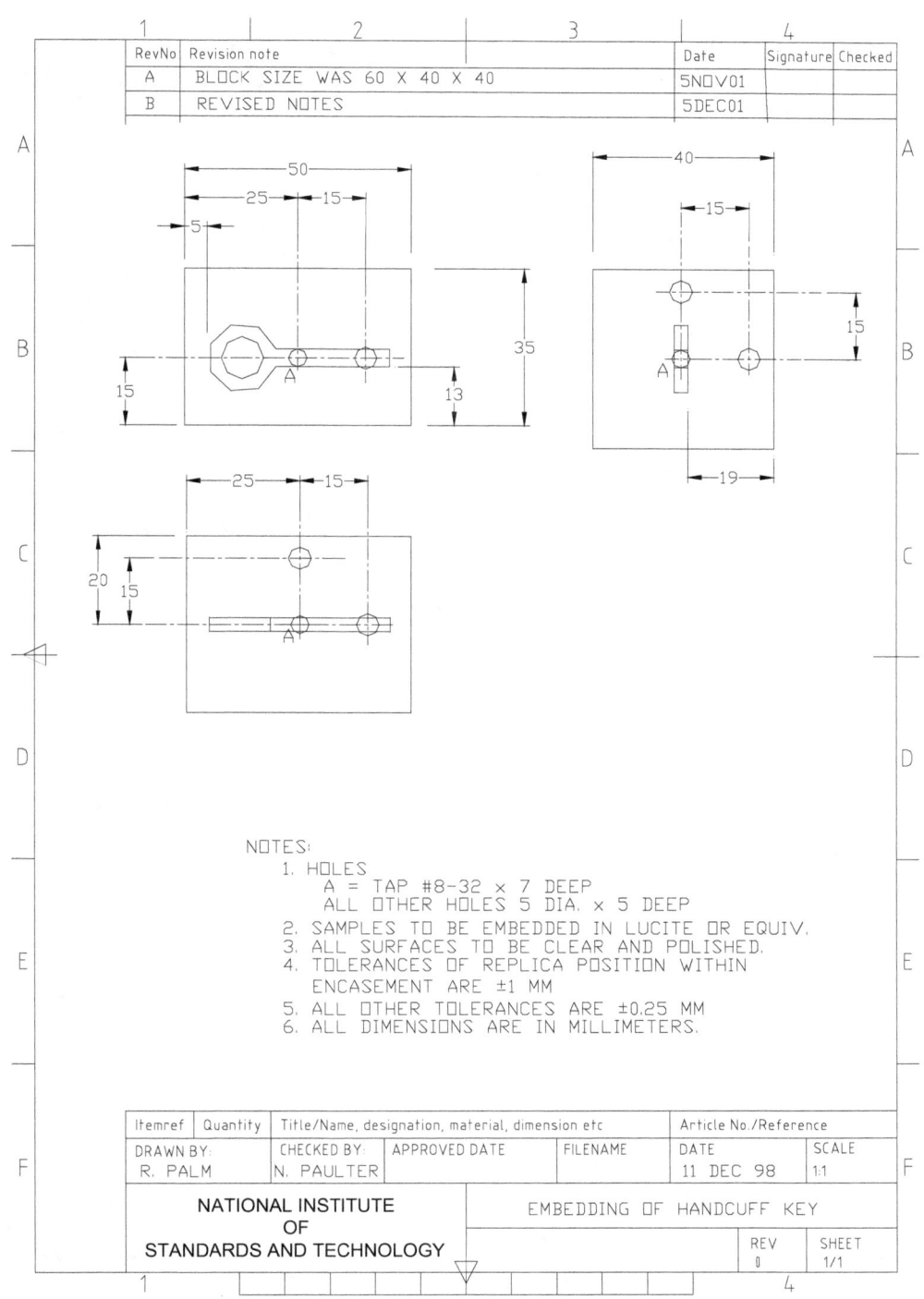

RevNo	Revision note	Date	Signature	Checked
A	BLOCK SIZE WAS 60 X 40 X 40	5NOV01		
B	REVISED NOTES	5DEC01		

NOTES:
1. HOLES
   A = TAP #8-32 x 7 DEEP
   ALL OTHER HOLES 5 DIA. x 5 DEEP
2. SAMPLES TO BE EMBEDDED IN LUCITE OR EQUIV.
3. ALL SURFACES TO BE CLEAR AND POLISHED.
4. TOLERANCES OF REPLICA POSITION WITHIN
   ENCASEMENT ARE ±1 MM
5. ALL OTHER TOLERANCES ARE ±0.25 MM
6. ALL DIMENSIONS ARE IN MILLIMETERS.

Itemref	Quantity	Title/Name, designation, material, dimension etc		Article No./Reference	
DRAWN BY: R. PALM	CHECKED BY: N. PAULTER	APPROVED DATE	FILENAME	DATE 11 DEC 98	SCALE 1:1

NATIONAL INSTITUTE OF STANDARDS AND TECHNOLOGY

EMBEDDING OF HANDCUFF KEY

REV 0 | SHEET 1/1

33

5.3.2 Nonferromagnetic Stainless Steel Knife

This section contains mechanical drawings of the replica of a nonferromagnetic stainless steel knife, a *small object size test object*. The mechanical drawings are arranged in the following order: the replica of the knife and the location of the replica within the encasement.

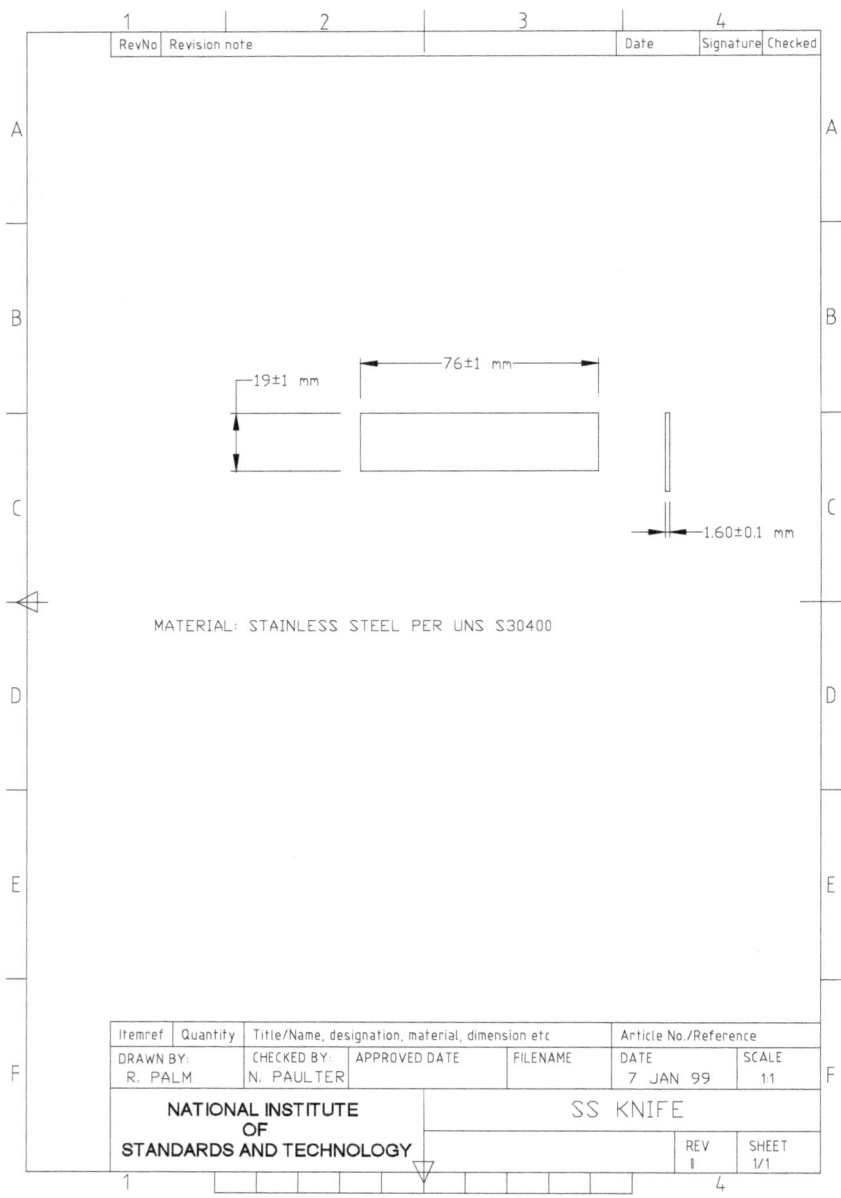

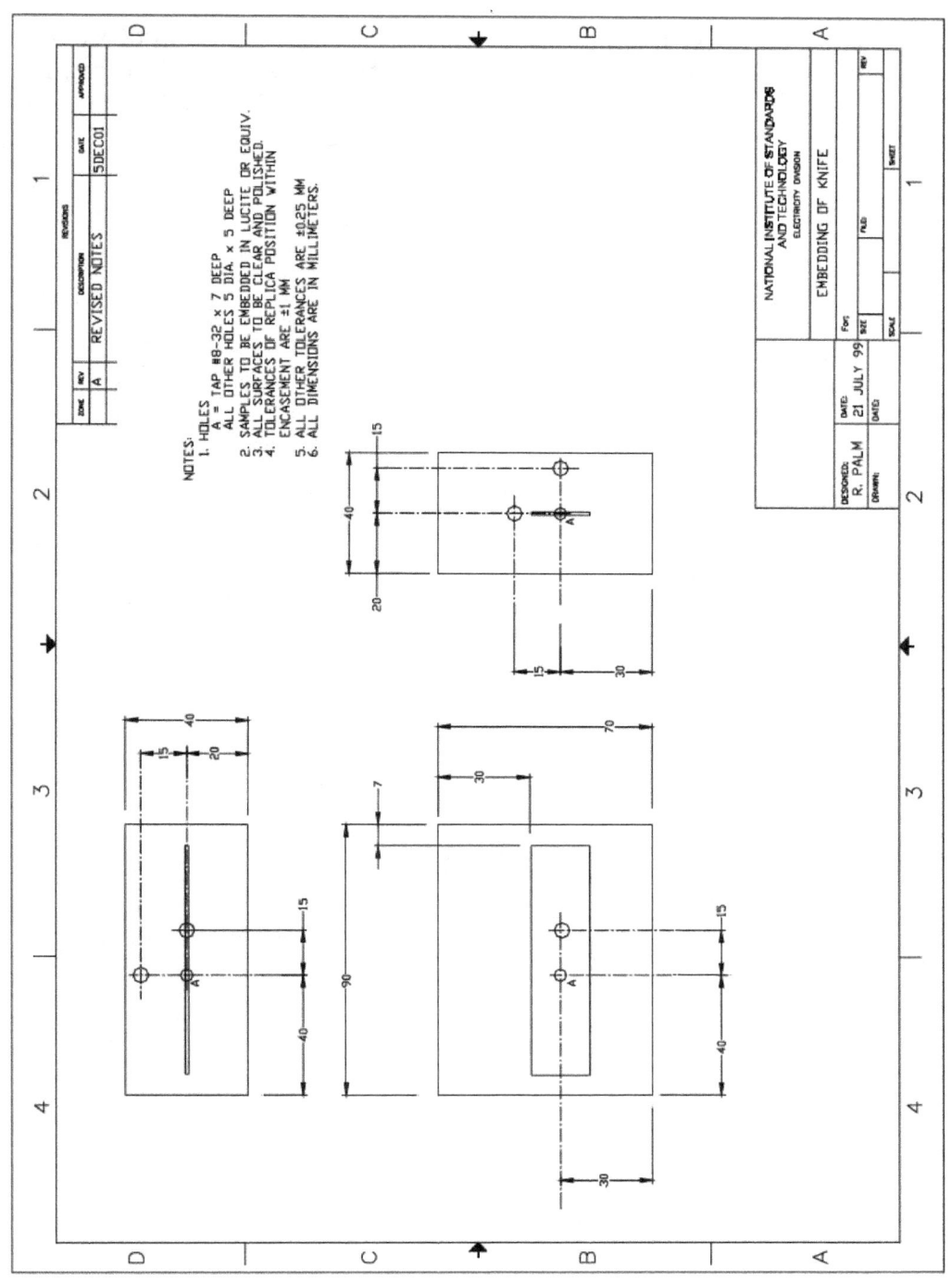

NOTES:
1. HOLES
   A = TAP #8-32 x 7 DEEP
   ALL OTHER HOLES 5 DIA x 5 DEEP
2. SAMPLES TO BE EMBEDDED IN LUCITE OR EQUIV.
3. ALL SURFACES TO BE CLEAR AND POLISHED.
4. TOLERANCES OF REPLICA POSITION WITHIN ENCASEMENT ARE ±1 MM
5. ALL OTHER TOLERANCES ARE ±0.25 MM
6. ALL DIMENSIONS ARE IN MILLIMETERS.

ZONE	REV	DESCRIPTION	DATE	APPROVED
	A	REVISED NOTES	5DEC01	

REVISIONS

NATIONAL INSTITUTE OF STANDARDS AND TECHNOLOGY
ELECTRICITY DIVISION

EMBEDDING OF KNIFE

DESIGNED: R. PALM
DRAWN:
DATE: 21 JULY 99
DATED:
FOR:
SIZE
SCALE
FILE:
SHEET
REV
1

5.3.3 Firearm Cartridge (22-Caliber Long Rifle)

This section contains mechanical drawings of the replica of a firearm cartridge, a *small object size test object.* The mechanical drawings are arranged in the following order: the cartridge assembly, the bullet portion of the replica, the case portion of the replica, and the location of the replica within the encasement.

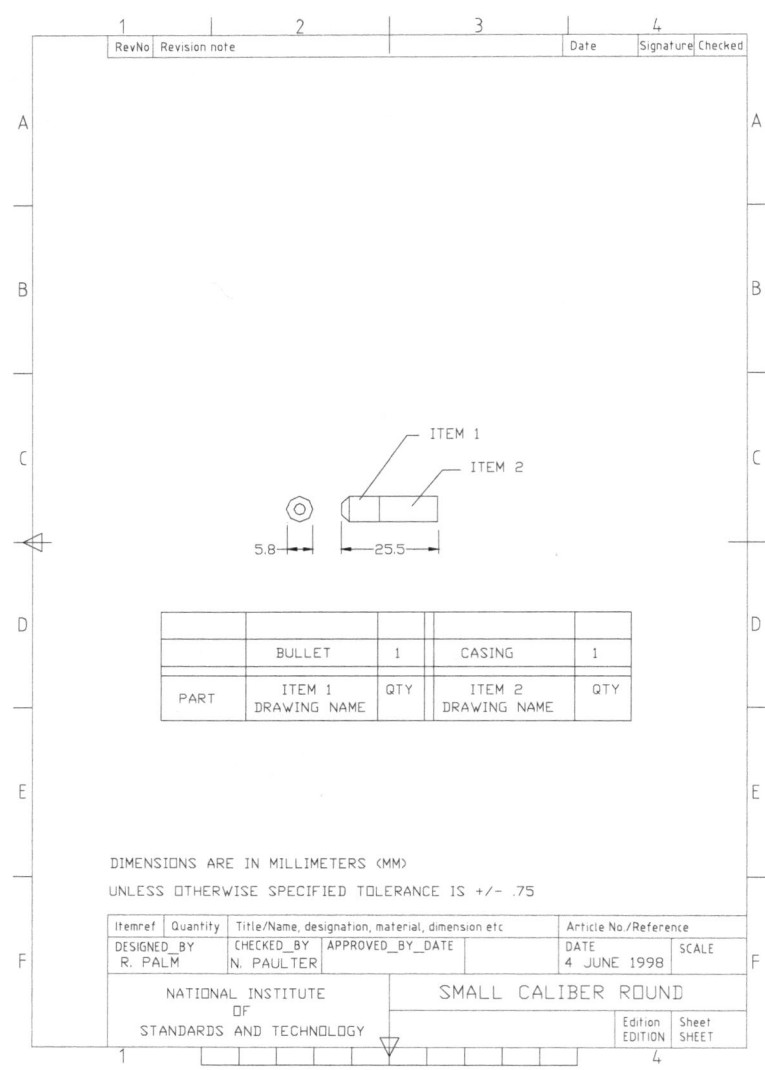

RevNo	Revision note				Date	Signature	Checked
		1	2	3		4	
A	REVISED SIZE				6/29/99		
B	REVISED MATERIAL SPEC.				7/19/01		

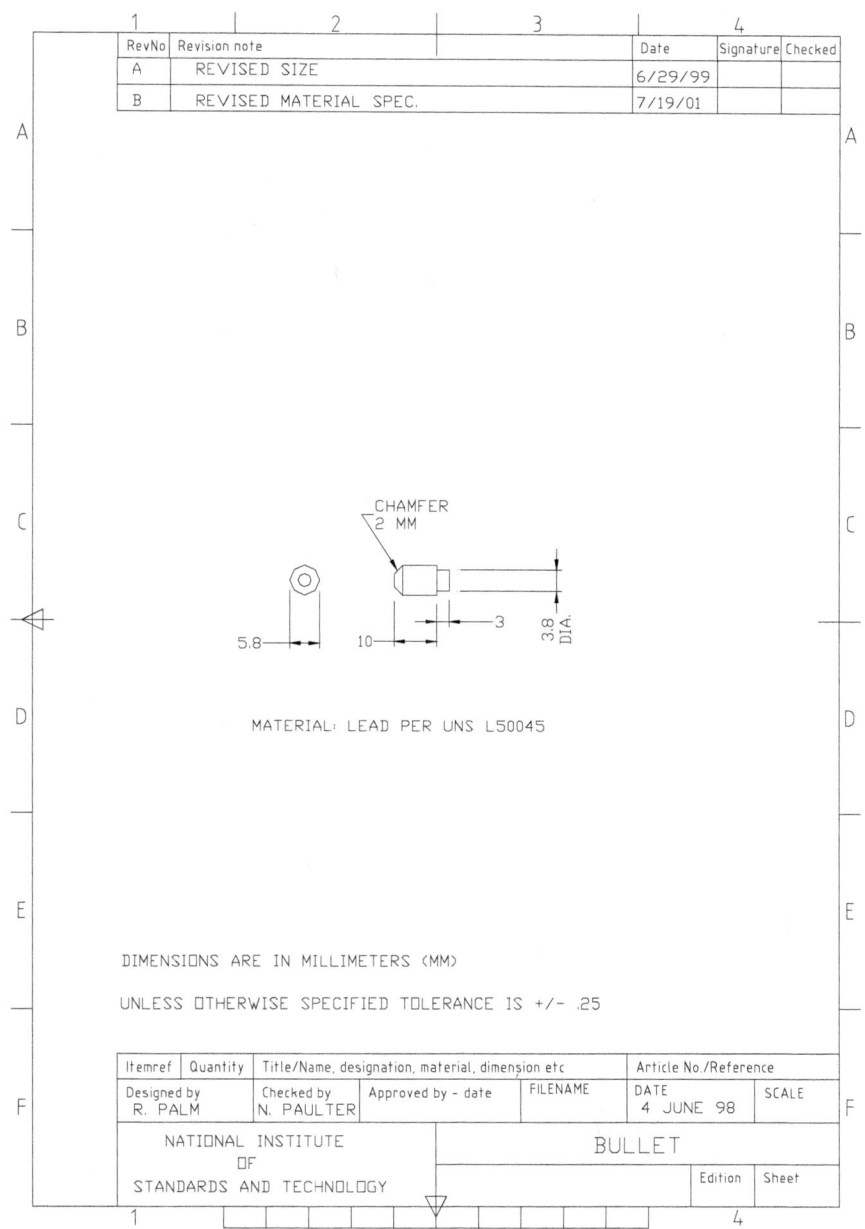

CHAMFER
2 MM

5.8

10

3

3.8 DIA.

MATERIAL: LEAD PER UNS L50045

DIMENSIONS ARE IN MILLIMETERS (MM)

UNLESS OTHERWISE SPECIFIED TOLERANCE IS +/- .25

Itemref	Quantity	Title/Name, designation, material, dimension etc		Article No./Reference		
Designed by R. PALM	Checked by N. PAULTER	Approved by - date	FILENAME	DATE 4 JUNE 98	SCALE	

NATIONAL INSTITUTE
OF
STANDARDS AND TECHNOLOGY

BULLET

Edition | Sheet

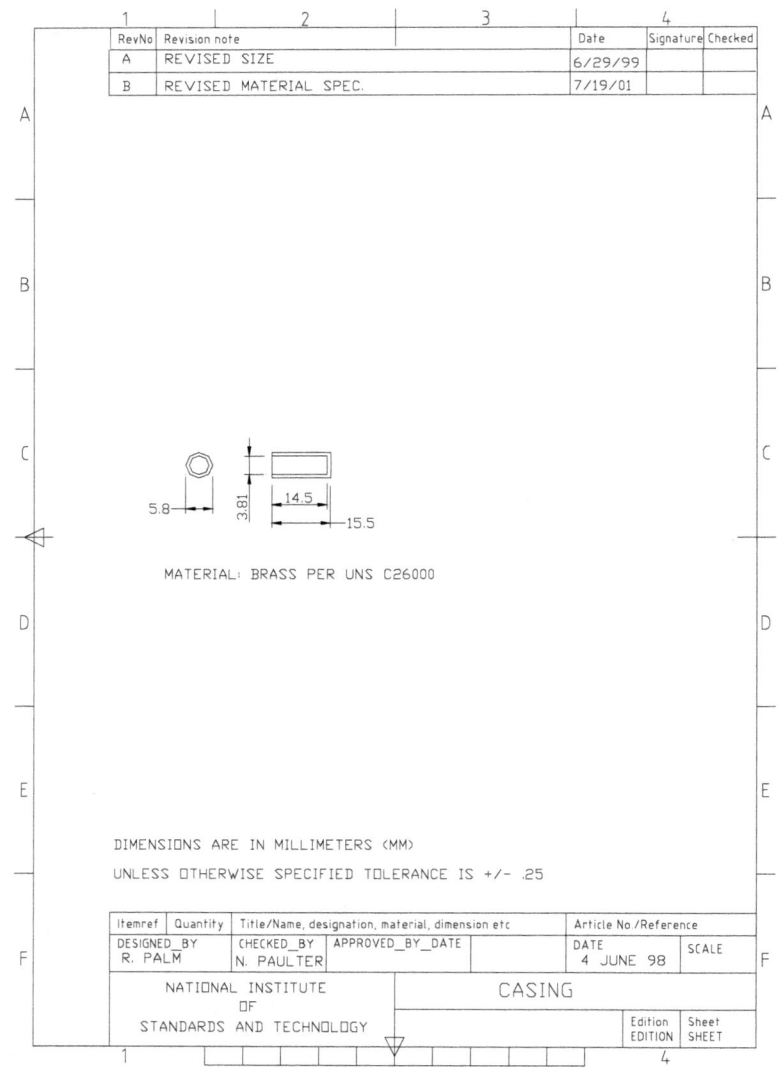

RevNo	Revision note			Date	Signature	Checked
A	REVISED SIZE			6/29/99		
B	REVISED MATERIAL SPEC.			7/19/01		

5.8   3.81   14.5   15.5

MATERIAL: BRASS PER UNS C26000

DIMENSIONS ARE IN MILLIMETERS (MM)

UNLESS OTHERWISE SPECIFIED TOLERANCE IS +/- .25

Itemref	Quantity	Title/Name, designation, material, dimension etc		Article No /Reference	
DESIGNED_BY R. PALM	CHECKED_BY N. PAULTER	APPROVED_BY_DATE		DATE 4 JUNE 98	SCALE

NATIONAL INSTITUTE
OF
STANDARDS AND TECHNOLOGY

CASING

| Edition EDITION | Sheet SHEET |

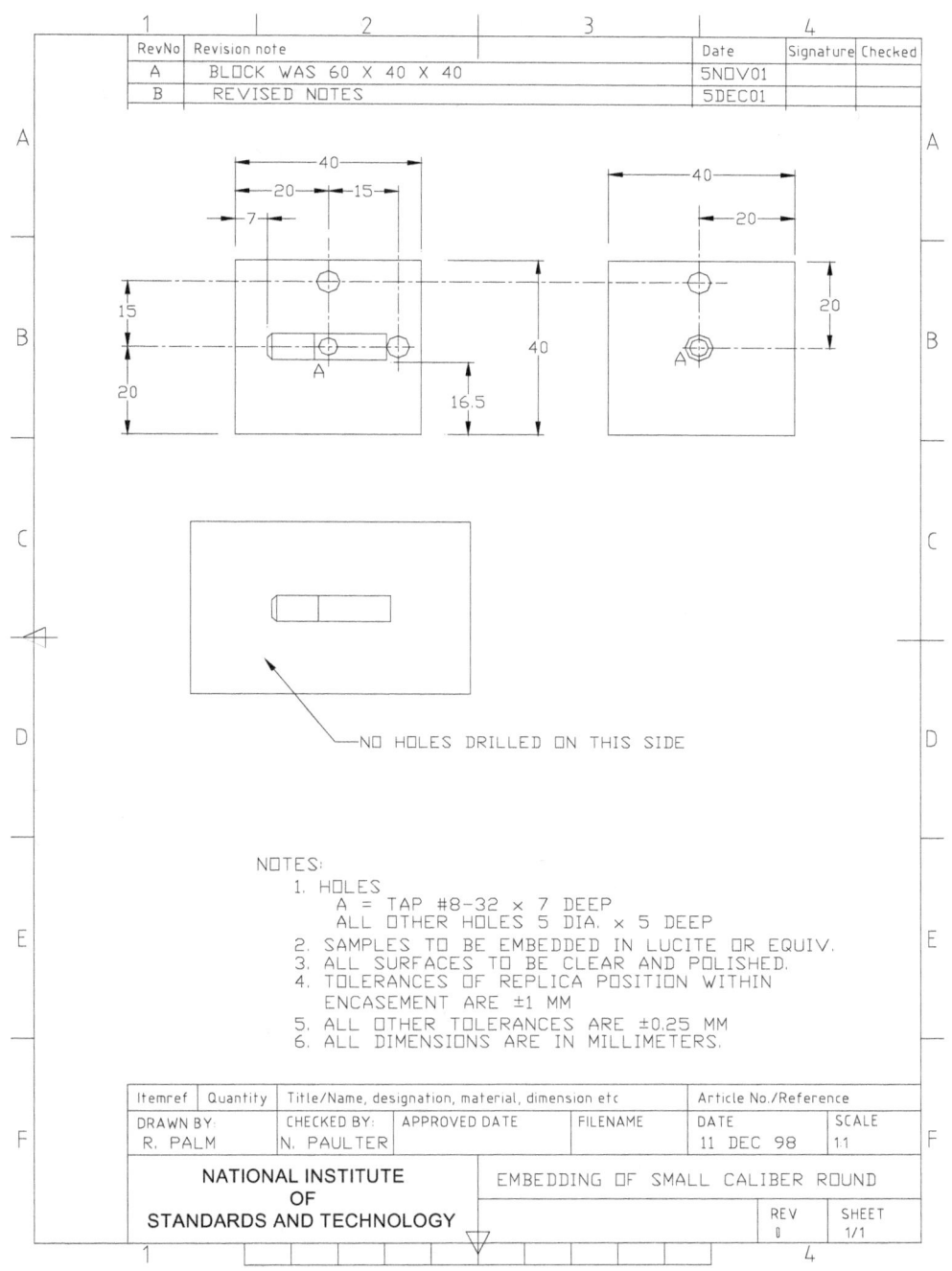

5.4 Very Small Object Size Test Objects

5.4.1 Pen Refill

This section contains mechanical drawings of the replica of a pen refill, a *very small object size test object*. The mechanical drawings are arranged in the following order: the replica of the pen refill and the location of the replica within the encasement.

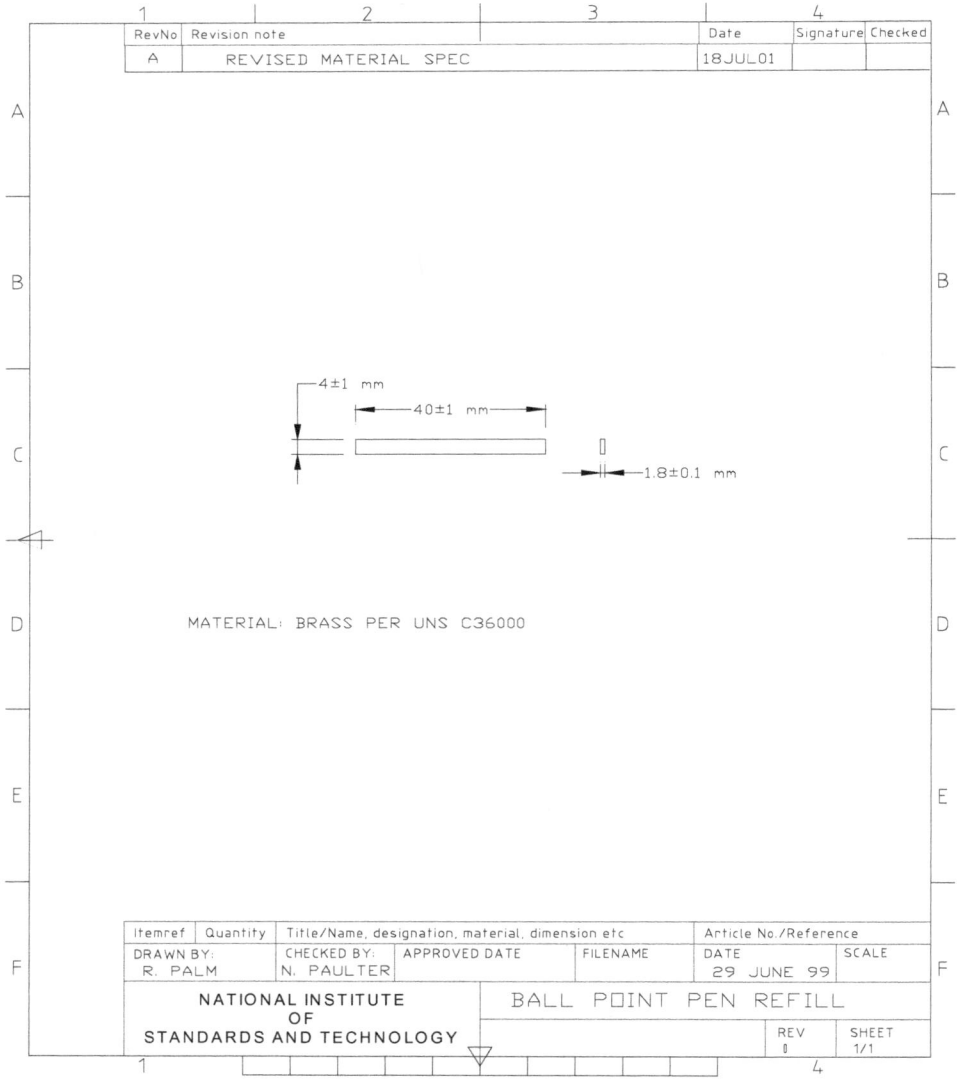

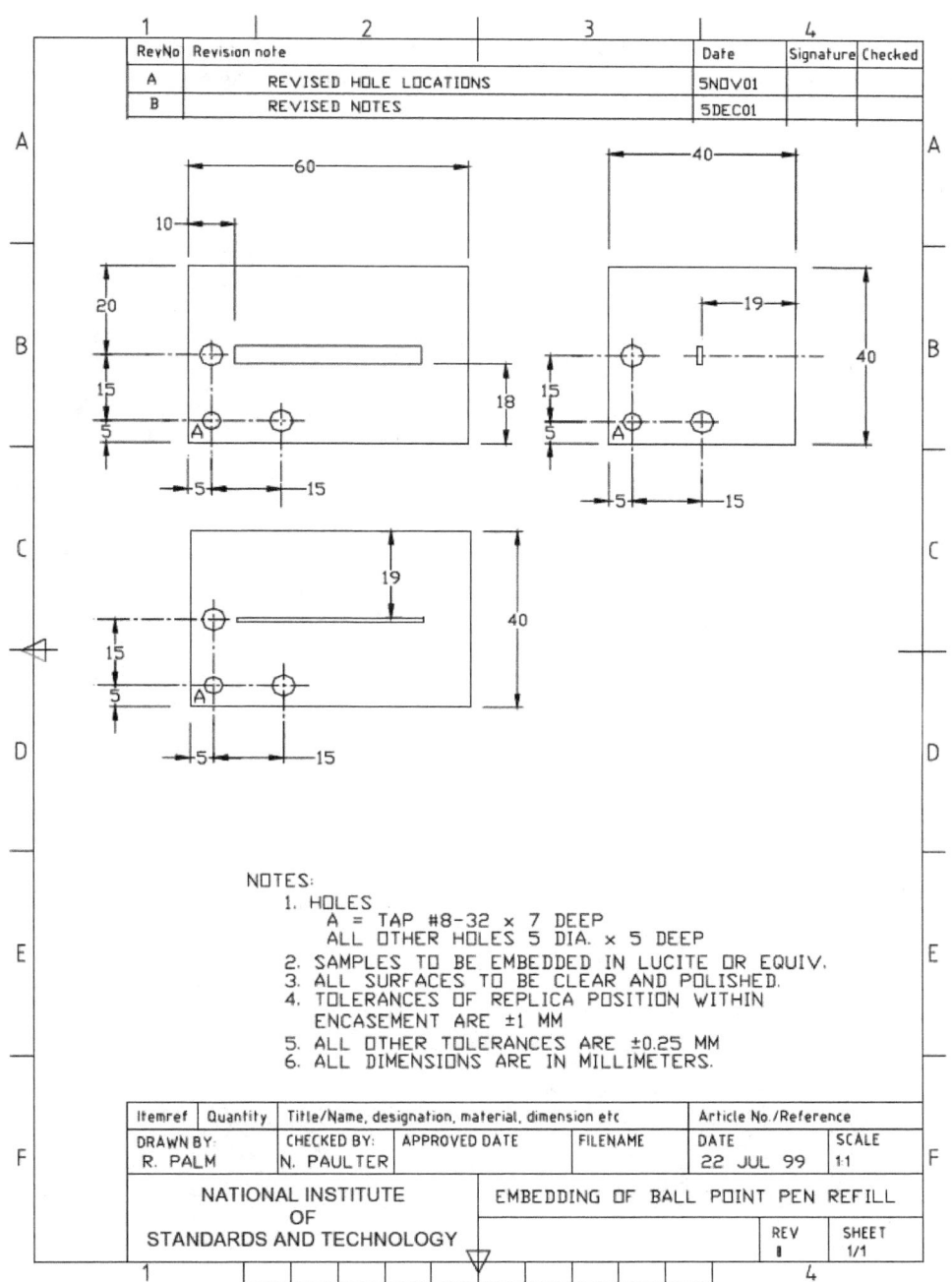

RevNo	Revision note			Date	Signature	Checked
A	REVISED HOLE LOCATIONS			5NOV01		
B	REVISED NOTES			5DEC01		

NOTES:
1. HOLES
   A = TAP #8-32 x 7 DEEP
   ALL OTHER HOLES 5 DIA. x 5 DEEP
2. SAMPLES TO BE EMBEDDED IN LUCITE OR EQUIV.
3. ALL SURFACES TO BE CLEAR AND POLISHED.
4. TOLERANCES OF REPLICA POSITION WITHIN
   ENCASEMENT ARE ±1 MM
5. ALL OTHER TOLERANCES ARE ±0.25 MM
6. ALL DIMENSIONS ARE IN MILLIMETERS.

Itemref	Quantity	Title/Name, designation, material, dimension etc		Article No./Reference	
DRAWN BY: R. PALM	CHECKED BY: N. PAULTER	APPROVED DATE	FILENAME	DATE 22 JUL 99	SCALE 1:1

NATIONAL INSTITUTE OF STANDARDS AND TECHNOLOGY

EMBEDDING OF BALL POINT PEN REFILL

REV B SHEET 1/1

5.4.2 Disposable Razor Blade

This section contains mechanical drawings of the replica of a disposable razor blade, a *very small object size test object*. The mechanical drawings are arranged in the following order: the replica of the razor blade and the location of the replica within the encasement.

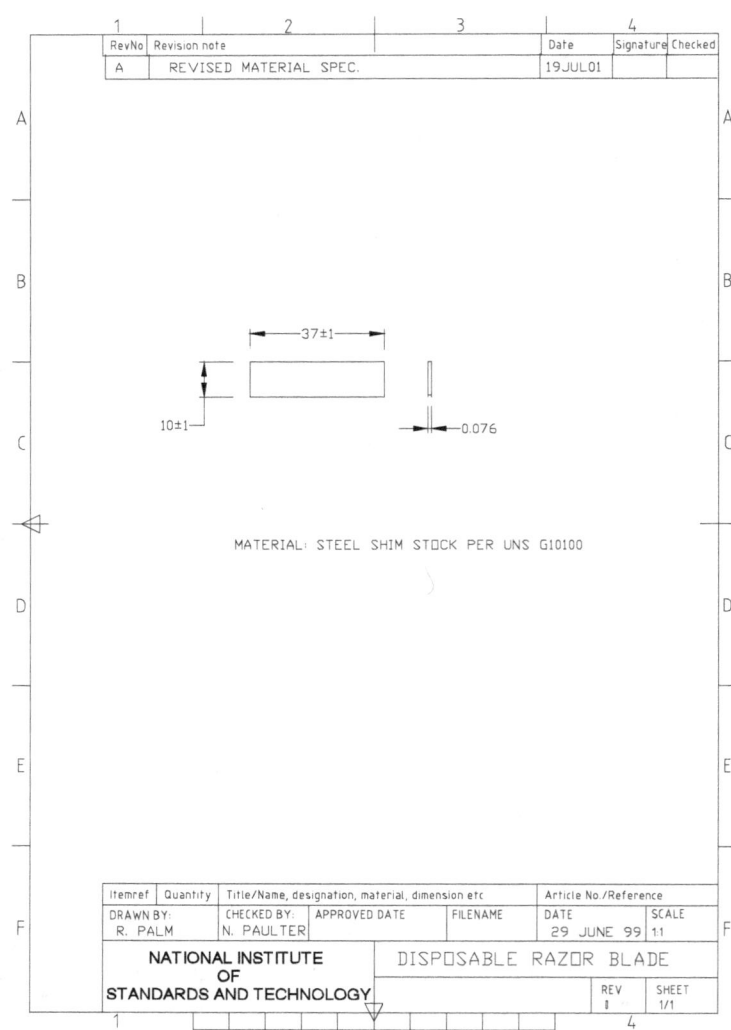

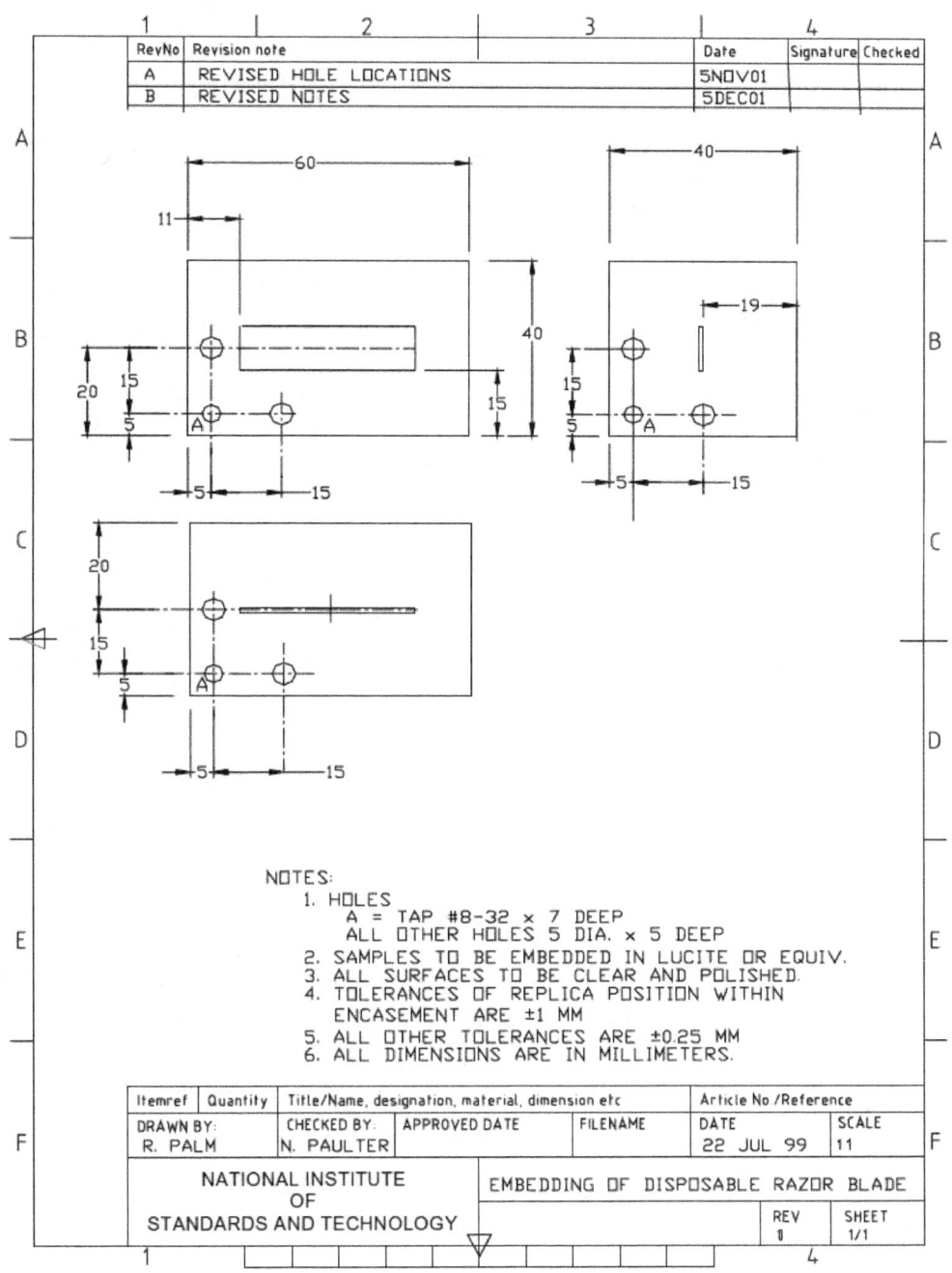

RevNo	Revision note			Date	Signature	Checked
A	REVISED HOLE LOCATIONS			5NOV01		
B	REVISED NOTES			5DEC01		

NOTES:
1. HOLES
   A = TAP #8-32 × 7 DEEP
   ALL OTHER HOLES 5 DIA. × 5 DEEP
2. SAMPLES TO BE EMBEDDED IN LUCITE OR EQUIV.
3. ALL SURFACES TO BE CLEAR AND POLISHED.
4. TOLERANCES OF REPLICA POSITION WITHIN
   ENCASEMENT ARE ±1 MM
5. ALL OTHER TOLERANCES ARE ±0.25 MM
6. ALL DIMENSIONS ARE IN MILLIMETERS.

Itemref	Quantity	Title/Name, designation, material, dimension etc		Article No /Reference		
DRAWN BY: R. PALM	CHECKED BY: N. PAULTER	APPROVED DATE	FILENAME	DATE 22 JUL 99	SCALE 11	

NATIONAL INSTITUTE
OF
STANDARDS AND TECHNOLOGY

EMBEDDING OF DISPOSABLE RAZOR BLADE

REV	SHEET
B	1/1

5.4.3 Hypodermic Needle, Disposable Syringe (Optional)

A mechanical drawing is not included because this is an optional *small object size test object*. It is suggested that the actual object be used for this optional *small object size test object*. This optional *test object* should be a stainless steel hypodermic needle with ferrule, typically found on disposable insulin syringes.

6. COMPLIANCE TEST REPORT FORM

The Compliance Test Report (CTR) form shall be used in conjunction with NIJ Standard 0602.02, *Hand-Held Metal Detectors for Use in Concealed Weapon and Contraband Detection*, and shall become a part of the official records of the compliance testing of each metal detector model submitted for testing. All sections of the form shall be completed.

An electronic file of the CTR form is available from the NLECTC Compliance Testing Office, National Law Enforcement and Corrections Technology Center-National (NLECTC-National). Requests for this file can be sent to: NLECTC-National, Attn: Metal Detector Testing Program, P.O. Box 1160, Rockville, MD 20849 1160; or by e-mail to asknlectc@nlectc.org.

7. REFERENCES

The following normative documents contain provisions, which through reference in this text, constitute provisions of this Standards Publication. By reference herein, these publications are adopted, in whole or in part, as indicated.

ANSI S1.4, 1971, American National Standards Institute, *Specifications for General Purpose Sound Level Meters.*

EN 50081 1 1992, European Standard, *Electromagnetic Compatibility - Generic Emission Standard, Part 1: Residential, Commercial, and Light Industry.*

EN 50082 1 1998, European Standard, *Electromagnetic Compatibility - Generic Immunity Standard, Part 1: Residential, Commercial, and Light Industry.*

IEC 68 2 27 1987, International Electrotechnical Commission, *Basic Environmental Testing Procedures, Part 2: Tests - Test Ea and Guidance: Shock.*

IEC 68 2 29 1987, International Electrotechnical Commission, *Basic Environmental Testing Procedures, Part 2: Tests - Test Eb and Guidance: Bump.*

IEC 68 2 32 1975, International Electrotechnical Commission, *Basic Environmental Testing Procedures, Part 2: Tests - Test Ed: Free Fall.*

IEC 60529 2001 2, International Electrotechnical Commission, *Degrees of Protection Provided by Enclosures (IP Code).*

IEEE C95.1 1991, Institute of Electrical and Electronic Engineers, *Standard for Safety Levels with Respect to Human Exposure to Radio Frequency Electromagnetic Fields, 3 kHz to 300 GHz.*

ISO 9001:2000, International Organization for Standardization 9001, *Quality Systems - Model for Quality Assurance in Design, Development, Production, Installation and Servicing.*

ISO 10012 1:1993 01 15, International Standards Organization, *Quality Assurance Requirements for Measuring Equipment, Part 1: Metrological Confirmation System for Measuring Equipment.*

ISO 10012 2:1997 09 15, International Standards Organization, *Quality Assurance for Measuring Equipment, Part 2: Guidelines for Control Measurement Process.*

ISO 17025:1999 12 15, International Standards Organization, *General Requirements for the Competence of Testing and Calibration Laboratories.*

MIL STD 461E Method RS101, Military Standard, *Requirements for the Control of Electromagnetic Interference Characteristics of Subsystems and Equipment, Method RS101, Radiated Susceptibility, Magnetic Field, 30 Hz to 100 kHz.*

MIL STD 810F Method 501.4, Military Standard, *Test Method Standard for Environmental Engineering Considerations and Laboratory Tests, Method 501.4, High Temperature.*

MIL STD 810F Method 502.4, Military Standard, *Test Method Standard for Environmental Engineering Considerations and Laboratory Tests, Method 502.4, Low Temperature.*

MIL STD 810F Method 505.4, Military Standard, *Test Method Standard for Environmental Engineering Considerations and Laboratory Tests, Method 505.4, Solar Radiation (Sunshine).*

MIL STD 810F Method 507.4, Military Standard, *Test Method Standard for Environmental Engineering Considerations and Laboratory Tests, Method 507.4, Humidity.*

MIL STD 810F Method 509.4, Military Standard, *Test Method Standard for Environmental Engineering Considerations and Laboratory Tests, Method 509.4, Salt Fog.*

NILECJ Standard 0602.00, National Institute of Law Enforcement and Criminal Justice, *Hand-Held Metal Detectors for Use in Weapons Detection.*

Safety Code, Recommended Safety Procedures for the Selection, Installation and Use of Active Metal Detectors, Radiation Protection Bureau, Canadian Minister of National Health and Welfare.

UL 60950, Underwriters Laboratories, *Safety for Information Technology Equipment.*

About the Law Enforcement and Corrections Standards and Testing Program

The Law Enforcement and Corrections Standards and Testing Program is sponsored by the Office of Science and Technology of the National Institute of Justice (NIJ), U.S. Department of Justice. The program responds to the mandate of the Justice System Improvement Act of 1979, which directed NIJ to encourage research and development to improve the criminal justice system and to disseminate the results to Federal, State, and local agencies.

The Law Enforcement and Corrections Standards and Testing Program is an applied research effort that determines the technological needs of justice system agencies, sets minimum performance standards for specific devices, tests commercially available equipment against those standards, and disseminates the standards and the test results to criminal justice agencies nationally and internationally.

The program operates through:

The *Law Enforcement and Corrections Technology Advisory Council* (LECTAC), consisting of nationally recognized criminal justice practitioners from Federal, State, and local agencies, which assesses technological needs and sets priorities for research programs and items to be evaluated and tested.

The *Office of Law Enforcement Standards* (OLES) at the National Institute of Standards and Technology, which develops voluntary national performance standards for compliance testing to ensure that individual items of equipment are suitable for use by criminal justice agencies. The standards are based upon laboratory testing and evaluation of representative samples of each item of equipment to determine the key attributes, develop test methods, and establish minimum performance requirements for each essential attribute. In addition to the highly technical standards, OLES also produces technical reports and user guidelines that explain in nontechnical terms the capabilities of available equipment.

The *National Law Enforcement and Corrections Technology Center* (NLECTC), operated by a grantee, which supervises a national compliance testing program conducted by independent laboratories. The standards developed by OLES serve as performance benchmarks against which commercial equipment is measured. The facilities, personnel, and testing capabilities of the independent laboratories are evaluated by OLES prior to testing each item of equipment, and OLES helps the NLECTC staff review and analyze data. Test results are published in Equipment Performance Reports designed to help justice system procurement officials make informed purchasing decisions.

Publications are available at no charge through the National Law Enforcement and Corrections Technology Center. Some documents are also available online through the Internet/World Wide Web. To request a document or additional information, call 800–248–2742 or 301–519–5060, or write:

National Law Enforcement and Corrections Technology Center
P.O. Box 1160
Rockville, MD 20849–1160
E-Mail: asknlectc@nlectc.org
World Wide Web address: http://www.nlectc.org